Broken Arrow #1

Broken Arrow #1

The World's First Lost Atomic Bomb

John Clearwater

hancock

house

ISBN 978-0-88839-596-2
Copyright © 2008 John M. Clearwater

Second printing 2010

Cataloging in Publication Data

Clearwater, John
    Broken arrow #1 : the world's first lost atomic bomb /
John M. Clearwater.

    Includes bibliographical references and index.
    ISBN 978-0-88839-596-2

    1. Nuclear weapons—Accidents—British Columbia—Pacific
Coast. 2. Atomic bomb—United States—History. 3. Aircraft accidents—British Columbia—Pacific Coast. I. Title.

U264.3.C57 2008   363.17'99'0916433   C2005-906572-9

Editor: Nancy Miller
Production: Mia Hancock, Ingrid Luters
Cover Design: Ingrid Luters
Front cover images: B-36B in flight.
Back cover images: Full-scale model of the Mk-4 atomic bomb on display at the Diefenbunker
Cold War Museum; crash site as it appeared in summer 2003; the explosives suitcase that held
the detonators; author John Clearwater.

*We acknowledge the financial support of the Government of Canada through the
Book Publishing Industry Development Program (BPIDP) for our publishing activities.*

Published simultaneously in Canada and the United States by

HANCOCK HOUSE PUBLISHERS LTD.
19313 Zero Avenue, Surrey, B.C. Canada V3S 9R9
(604) 538-1114 Fax (604) 538-2262

HANCOCK HOUSE PUBLISHERS
1431 Harrison Avenue, Blaine, WA U.S.A. 98230-5005
(604) 538-1114 Fax (604) 538-2262

Website: **www.hancockhouse.com**
Email: **sales@hancockhouse.com**

Contents

Acknowledgments

As this book came about due to my involvement with a documentary and museum expedition, and as a result of being the curator of the *Lost Nuke* museum exhibit, there are several people who need to be acknowledged.

The *Lost Nuke* exhibit was made possible by generous sponsorship from Discovery Channel Canada and the Alberta Aviation Museum in Edmonton. The artifacts were provided courtesy of the Diefenbunker, Canada's Cold War Museum in Ottawa. Allison Fletcher was the exhibit designer, and Proulx Bros. of Ottawa produced the images.

The 2003 expedition to the crash site had three team members: James Laird of Vancouver, Dirk Septer from British Columbia, and myself. The film crew from MythMerchant Films, which captured the highs and lows of the expedition, was led by Michael Jorgensen with support from Igal Petel and Michael Carroll. Most importantly, I have to acknowledge the role played by Michael Jorgensen, the filmmaker for MythMerchant Films. It was Michael who brought together the film project and who made me think very intensely about this subject. It has been my pleasure to know and work with Michael for nearly five years, and I hope someday to make a film under his guidance.

All photographs used in this book are courtesy of the author; the Diefenbunker, Canada's Cold War Museum; the Department of National Defence; the U.S. Department of Defense; the RCMP; the *Vancouver Province*; and the *Vancouver Sun*.

Author's Explanation and Caveat

The events described in this book are among the first of the modern nuclear age. They were secretly inscribed on the first pages of the book of the nuclear era but were never to be known to any but an elite and highly cleared cadre of nuclear weapons specialists.

The loss of a nuclear weapon has always been occasion for governments to enact great cover-ups, issue false stories or not to say anything at all. The world's first lost atomic bomb was a bit different, as in 1950 there was no expectation of public information, and the bomb was lost without civilian witnesses. The crew was simply debriefed by the U.S. government and the matter was classified, as all other matters were at the time.

Many people have concluded from this secrecy that a grand cover-up was put in place to hide some deeper truth about the whole incident. Some have suggested that the bomb crashed in the interior of British Columbia. Others say that it was a live atomic bomb. Still others believe that the plane flew all the way to Vancouver Island before returning to crash far to the north. Whatever the theory, the whole idea rests on the supposition that a vast conspiracy, often involving both the U.S. and Canadian governments, is still at work.

In order to explain the conspiracy, many have asserted that the written record is nothing but a tissue of lies. Some have said that the entire declassified record is false and does nothing other than cover-up the truth about the world's first "Broken Arrow."

It is my belief, based on a review of the records and the incident, that there is in fact no conspiracy to cover up what happened over the coast of northern British Columbia in February 1950. The documentary record that some claim is faked is nothing of the kind. Although it seems at times inconsistent, it should not in fact be doubted on that basis. It is in fact a compilation of what were perceived as truths at the time by different people in charge of different parts of the mission and the investigation.

While it may seem unusual that the crash investigators were not allowed to speak of the atomic aspects of the mission, it is hardly a sign of a conspiracy of silence. This was merely a sign of good security planning and execution. These people had no clearance to know or talk about nuclear matters.

"There's still things that I can't talk about, that I won't talk about."

— *S/Sgt. Dick Thrasher, Gunner*

The idea that these fifty-year-old documents are part of an elaborate cover-up misses a crucial fact: the documents were never meant to be seen by anyone outside of the USAF and the Atomic Energy Agency. These records were to remain a secret forever. And there is no good reason to falsify secret records that cannot be viewed by any but the most highly cleared personnel, a small group of people indeed.

All the documentation was written before the advent of the Freedom of Information Act (FOIA), which would pry open a small selection of documents decades later. Had FOIA not become law, these records would still be a secret. There was no reason to falsify records that were to always be a secret.

Some conspiracy theorists have concluded that the official story is false, based on so-called eyewitness testimony from people on the ground. A total lack of verifiable testimony from identifiable people willing to make public statements has completely undermined this avenue of research. Statements made years after the fact are very often blurred with information gleaned from readings and media presentations, as well as an understandable desire to have something important to say about an event. I call this the History Channel syndrome, in which people add into their memory things learned long after the actual event. Such statements are all but useless for historical purposes, but do tell us a great deal about what people thought, as well as how they saw and see events and their place in them.

Given that the declassified military record is probably of reasonably good accuracy, I conclude that the bomber lost power and altitude and that the crew dropped the unarmed (non-nuclear-cored) Mk-4 atomic bomb over the Pacific Ocean very near the B.C. coast before they bailed out over Princess Royal Island. The bomber then somehow (and I do not know how) managed to fly to a point higher than the bailout altitude, where it crashed into the peak of a mountain range.

This is still quite a story, and one that remains shrouded in mystery. There is indeed a nuclear weapon involved, and it did have at least forty kilograms of depleted uranium inside, although no plutonium core. The flight to the crash site cannot be explained, but that only adds to the value of the story.

Since I have been misquoted in the press, it is important for readers to note that I believe there was a nuclear weapon on the aircraft and that this weapon was jettisoned far closer to the Canadian coast than reported by official documents. This has been proven to be true in the case of the Mk-43 lost in the Sea of Japan; it was far closer to Japan than reported.

In the spring of 2000, I was contacted by Michael Jorgensen of MythMerchant Films in Edmonton. He is the now-famous maker of the Emmy-award winning documentary *Battle of the X-Planes* for PBS Nova. Mike was interested in making a film about a lost nuclear weapon and asked me to look into several so that we could choose the incident best-suited for a film. I did some basic research, and during the summer we met on board the RMS *Queen Mary* in Long Beach, California, to discuss the project's direction. We decided that the world's first Broken Arrow, as the wreckage was on land in northern B.C., would be ideal from the viewpoint of film logistics and finances.

For the next three years we slowly researched and prepared the story and script. Additional documents were gathered, and Mike brought on two others with some interesting knowledge of the event.

In August 2003, I led a museum expedition into the mountains to view the crash site of aircraft 92075. With the first-ever government permit issued for exploration and recovery of artifacts from the wreckage, a team of three specialists and a film crew of three from MythMerchant Films spent a week with the remains of the B-36 bomber.

What you will read here is the generally accepted version of events based on the best document research and site investigation available. There are other versions of events, but most are unsupportable by hard evidence. Should new and verifiable documentary evidence become available as a result of further declassification, I am willing to change my view of the events of February 13–14, 1950.

Although we made no discoveries that would change the view of history, we learned a great deal. What follows is a summation of what we know now with greater certainty than ever before. That said, whatever errors or omissions contained herein are my fault alone.

This book was written to most closely reflect the exact facts with as little embellishment as possible. Where able and appropriate, exact quotes are used and they have been reproduced in their original format. Exceptions are noted in square where explanations or conversions were required. The documents reproduced in the appendices at the back of the book are in their original wording and format; again any additions or explanations are noted with square brackets.

— Dr. John Murray Clearwater

Introduction

Broken Arrow: a nuclear weapon that has been lost, or is in danger of exploding or has exploded. It covers the theft, seizure or intentional dropping of nuclear weapons short of war.

On a simulated bombing mission, a new B-36 bomber from Strategic Air Command experienced catastrophic engine failures on three of its six engines. Before the bomber crashed into a mountainside, the crew reportedly dropped their atomic bomb over the Pacific Ocean in Hecate Strait.

The aircraft used by the 7th Heavy Bombardment Wing stationed at Carswell Air Force Base, Fort Worth, Texas, was carrying one of the first two Mark-4 atomic bombs ever loaned to the U.S. Air Force by the Atomic Energy Commission. The other was in a sister aircraft flying a similar mission.

The aircraft was prepared for a twenty-four-hour flight and, in addition to a very heavy atomic bomb, carried twenty-eight hours worth of fuel. The training mission called on the crew to fly from Eielson, Alaska, practice bombing San Francisco and then fly home to their base in Texas. They were testing procedures for operating with atomic weapons from far northern bases.

The weather on the flight path was unfavorable. High velocity winds came from the southeast. Icing conditions were scattered throughout the flight path. Although the pilot knew about the bad weather, he was unaware of the fact that ice could build up on an aircraft in the far north.

The crew departed at 4:27 p.m.; seven hours into the flight, ice buildup caused surging in all six engines and fires ignited in three of them.

To preserve the secret of the atomic bomb, it had to be destroyed. U.S. Air Force records show the B-36 headed out over the Pacific and dropped the bomb. The crew reported that the Mk-4 atomic bomb lit up the sky north-northwest of Princess Royal Island, British Columbia.

As soon as the bomber was over land, and possibly within sight of Mount Cardin, the crew parachuted toward Princess Royal Island. Twelve of the seventeen airmen survived and were rescued within three days.

The massive bomber's autopilot was set on a course of 190 degrees, which would fly the bomber south-southwest where it would safely crash at sea. Instead, it circled over the heads of the crew and flew north-northeast.

The U.S. military, very concerned about the loss of seventeen crew members, one bomber and one atomic bomb, immediately launched a huge search operation. The crew men were rescued by fishermen and the Royal Canadian Navy, but the aircraft was not found.

When the bomber was discovered three years later, a U.S. military special operations team was sent in to ensure that no secret equipment could be retrieved.

With the crew rescued, the mystery began.

Chapter 1: The Nuclear World in 1950

The Cold War

"The Russians are frightened and the Yanks are bomb-minded."

— Ernest Bevin, U.K. Foreign Secretary,
1946, at the Paris Peace Conference

The Cold War (1945–1991) was a political fight by the United States against an enemy in the form of Soviet communism. For the U.S.S.R., the Cold War was a means to manage the Stalinist empire, justified by the threat from capitalism and the Pentagon.

The Cold War was a time of nonmilitary global conflict. People were cowed with fear, and paranoia swept entire populations. Red-blooded Americans were urged to seek out communist subversion wherever it might be. Good Soviet citizens were constantly told to be vigilant in the face of imperialism and the agents of the dark forces.

With the exception of the Cuban Missile Crisis in 1962, there was not a single direct national military confrontation between the superpowers during the entire Cold War. On a combat level, Soviet pilots did replace less-skilled North Korean pilots in the Korean War, and U.S. pilots replaced Cuban mercenaries during the Bay of Pigs invasion. In general, military combat by the U.S.S.R. was limited to their border areas. The United States intervened worldwide in an attempt to extend and solidify its position as the only truly global superpower.

In the United States, the Cold War was used to support the growing military-industrial complex through massive tax subsidies. In the U.S.S.R., the Cold War allowed the bureaucratic-military ruling class, often called the "steel-eaters" (due to their emphasis on heavy industry and military production), to become even more firmly established in power.

Each side used the other to justify military actions in their own external spheres and to scare and control their own populations by terrifying them with the horrific crimes of the other.

In 1949 the U.S.S.R. was ruled by Stalin and the U.S.A. by Truman. Revolution had swept Mao's communists to power in China; but British and U.S. intervention had destroyed a communist-led movement in Greece. The U.S. Marshall Plan for the redevelopment of Europe purposely excluded the U.S.S.R., and in turn the Soviets tried to strangle West Berlin and force out the other allies. Canada, the United States and ten western European countries formed the North Atlantic Treaty Organization (NATO) as a way of providing political and emotional support to Western Europe in competition with the U.S.S.R. The Soviet Union then tested its first atomic bomb in August, four years after the United States.

It was in this secretive and paranoid world that a crew of seventeen men flew that cold night in February 1950.

The Nuclear Balance

By the beginning of 1950, the United States had approximately 234 atomic bombs. The arsenal was made up of the obsolete and inefficient Little Boy bomb, the awkward Fat Man bomb and the new Mk-4 atomic bomb. The Mk-5 and Mk-6 bomb were about to come into service.

Just as important as the weapons themselves was the delivery force. The United States had built a large, heavy bomber force capable of delivering even the heaviest atomic bomb to a target inside the U.S.S.R. They had also built a series of bases and airfields around the world from which they could launch attacks with bombers.

The U.S.S.R. had just tested an atomic bomb in late August 1949 (Semipalatinsk-21, Kazakhstan) and it is likely they had one or two functional atomic bombs. Testimony from scientists revealed they tested a copy of the U.S. Fat Man bomb in order to keep Beria and the Soviet secret police satisfied while they developed a more powerful and efficient weapon for later testing.

The Soviet Union had no way of actually delivering an atomic bomb to any target inside the continental United States. They lacked a true long-range air force and would not have this capability for several years. Even their copied B-29 bombers could not reach U.S. targets other than Alaska from inside the U.S.S.R. The Soviets never built overseas airbases for bomber operations.

Strategic Air Command

Strategic Air Command was established on 21 March 1946, as one of the three major combat commands of the United States Army Air Forces, with General George C. Kenney as commander. SAC was to make war with "long range offensive operations employing the latest and most advanced weapons."

The first mission of SAC, as issued by the chief of the Army Air Force, was as follows: "The Strategic Air Command will be prepared to conduct long range offensive operations in any part of the world either independently or in cooperation with land and Naval forces; to conduct maximum range reconnaissance over land or sea either independently or in cooperation with land and Naval forces; to provide combat units capable of intense and sustained combat operations employing the latest and most advanced weapons; to train units and personnel for the maintenance of the Strategic Forces in all parts of the world; to perform such special missions as the Commanding General, Army Air Forces may direct."

The first test attempts to use SAC aircraft in a bombing mode saw a small number of B-29s "attack" Los Angeles on 11 April 1947. Two weeks later, 101 of the bombers attacked New York City in a practice "maximum effort mission." In the early years of the Cold War, SAC planners envisioned B-36s operating westward from forward locations in Alaska and Okinawa. Although rotational training at these two bases had ceased in 1948, they were still included in SAC's war plan. In late 1948, SAC had a new war plan, "Trojan," which called for B-36 mis-

Strategic Air Command emblem.
Credit: U.S. Air Force

sions to be generated from U.S. bases. Trojan emphasized a powerful first strike in an intense strategic air offensive and was approved as the official war plan in January 1949.

Curtis LeMay became SAC commander on 19 October 1948, and SAC headquarters moved to Nebraska from Maryland the following month. LeMay's job was to whip SAC into a fighting force. By the end of 1949, Secretary of the Air Force Stuart Symington said that, "existence of this strategic atomic striking force is the greatest deterrent in the world today to the start of another global war." He was also lobbying for an increase in the air force budget, which in 1949 was very unlikely.

In December 1949, only two months before the accident, SAC had 10,050 officers, 53,460 airmen and 7,980 civilian personnel. The force had 868 aircraft: 390 B-29 bombers, 36 B-36 bombers, 99 B-50 bombers, 67 KB-29 tankers, 62 RB-29 reconnaissance aircraft, and 18 RB-17 reconnaissance aircraft. The bombers were divided into three heavy bomb groups with eighteen aircraft each; one group was equipped with a B-36 and the other two were outfitted with the new bomber. Remaining bombers were divided into eleven medium bomb groups of B-29 and B-50 aircraft. SAC also had eighteen atomic assembly teams. Operationally, crews were issued targeting material for about half their targets inside the U.S.S.R.

Under the command of Lieutenant General Curtis E. LeMay and deputy commander Major General Thomas S. Power, SAC now had seventeen bases in the continental United States. The proficiency of SAC combat crews was atrocious in the early years, so LeMay instituted the "lead crew" system to improve bombing scores. First used in World War II, the system saw select lead crews trained at Walker AFB in the U.S.

SAC's real problem was personnel. There was a nationwide reenlistment problem: almost nobody stayed in the military. During the first massive call-up for Korea, most of the pilots and observers recalled to active duty with SAC had flown bombers in World War II. They largely did not want to fly again for the military, and there was popular discontent.

The new nuclear war plan the United States had in early 1950, "Dropshot," called for SAC to drop 300 atomic weapons on 200 Soviet and Chinese cities. Ironically, this was impossible, since

SAC Commander in Chief General Curtis LeMay (left), Senator Russell, General Roger M. Ramey, Major John Bartlett, Air Force Secretary Symington, Senator (later president) Lyndon Johnson (second from right), and Representative Thornberry with a B-36B bomber from the same unit as aircraft #075 on 19 November 1949.
Credit: U.S. Air Force

there were far fewer bombs in the U.S. arsenal at the time, but this fact was unknown to the war planners.

The first true exercise of the entire nuclear delivery system came in June 1950 with Exercise Becalm. Starting on 4 June, the force was alerted and, with the participation of the Atomic Energy Commission, picked up weapons at the storage depots and flew concerted "attacks" with sixty atomic bombers and 104 other bombers against sites in the U.S. representing Soviet targets. It was thought that fifty-eight of the sixty reached their targets and dropped their bombs.

By the end of February 1951, the U.S. had stopped the enemy advance in southern Korea, but there were rumors of a Chinese attack. Truman warned Congress that the U.S. might widen the war and that, if necessary, he would authorize the transfer of atomic weapons to military custody. Truman eventually allowed nine bombs and nine cores to be sent to Guam, but not until April 1951. The cores were withdrawn back to AEC custody later in the year.

SAC's supplier of nuclear weapons was the Atomic Energy Commission, but the weapons were now being held by the Armed

Forces Special Weapons Project for the time being. In October, 1951, the AFSWP became the Special Weapons Center with a largely air force staff. Truman approved a report on 10 September 1952 that appeared to take the momentous step of giving the armed services full control of the weapons in the stockpile. However, no executive order followed the acceptance of the report, and even Eisenhower did not sign in 1953. Administrative custody of the weapons remained with the AEC throughout the 1950s.

B-36B Heavy Bomber

The B-36 was the world's first true intercontinental bomber, carrying conventional or nuclear bombs from the U.S.A. to Europe and beyond. Its first test flight was on 8 August 1945, right between the Hiroshima and Nagasaki atomic bombings.

The massive aircraft was an interim bomber between the limited range B-29 propeller aircraft of World War II and the new B-52 jet bomber of the 1950s. In 1947 a B-36 set a world long-distance record by flying 15,440 kilometers (9,590 miles) in 43.5 hours without refueling. The USAF accepted 385 bombers, including the initial test aircraft. Despite deliveries in the late 1940s, due to the almost constant series of modifications the B-36 was not considered a fully operational bomber until 1952.

The SAC bombing competition of 1949 showed that a B-36B unit scored best with a visual bombing accuracy of 135 meters (441 ft.) from 7,600 meters (25,000 ft.) altitude. They could radar bomb with an accuracy of 320 meters (1,053 ft.).

Convair of Texas, U.S.A., built seventy-three B-36B aircraft, of which four were delivered as B-36Ds, and seven as RB-36Ds (reconnaissance craft). Production ended in September 1950, with the delivery of the sixty-second B-36B. Phase out began in the first half of 1951 when the first twenty-five aircraft were returned to the manufacturer to be converted to D models. A major problem was encountered with the new engines. The R-4360-41 engines in the B-36B demanded extra fuel tanks. The new bomb bay tanks, which were supposedly self-sealing, leaked throughout the entire service life of the bomber.

The Convair Company built sixty-two B-36Bs in 1949 and 1950, at a cost of $2.5 million each. The average B-36 cost $3.63

B-36B in flight. *Credit: Convair & U.S. Air Force.*

Type: B-36B

Crew: 15

Wingspan: 70.4 m

Length: 49.6 m

Height: 14.4 m

Maximum Weight: 186 tonnes

Maximum bomb load: 39 tonnes of nuclear or conventional bombs

Nuclear Weapons: MkIII, Mk-4, Mk-5, Mk-6, Mk-17, Mk-21, B-36, B-39

Engines: six Pratt & Whitney R-4360-41 Wasp Major air-cooled engines

Maximum speed: 610 km/h

Cruising speed: 325 km/h

Range: 42.5 hours, 17,000 km unrefueled

Service Ceiling: 13,900 m

Total Mission Time: 42:43 hours

Mission Aircraft

Aircraft No. 44-92075

Type, model, series: B-36B

Home station: Carswell Air Force Base, Fort Worth, Texas

Command: SAC

Subcommand: 8th AF

Wing: 7th Bomb Wing

Group No. and type: 7th Bomb Group (Heavy)

Squadron: 436th Bomb Squadron

Date of Manufacture: 31 July 1949

Total flight hours: 185:25

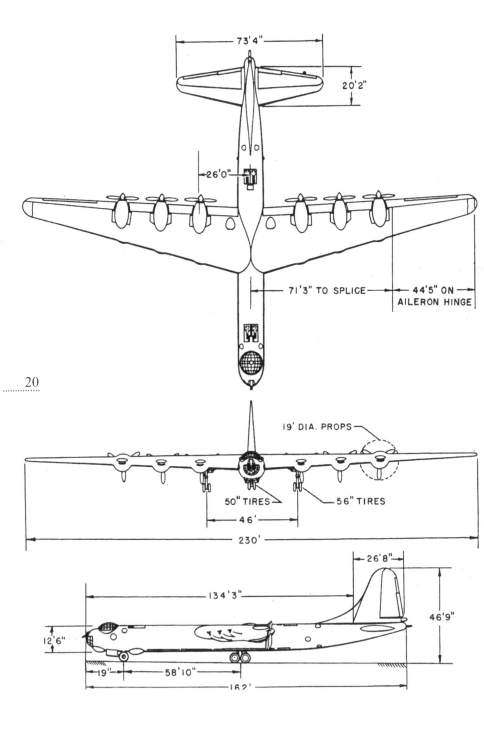

B-36 general layout three-way view of aircraft. *Credit: U.S. Air Force*

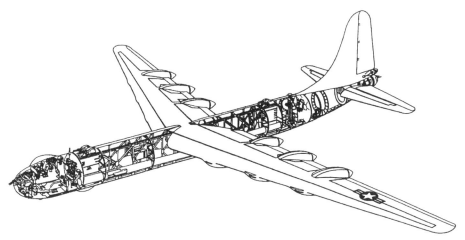

Fuselage cutaway of a B-36B. *Credit: U.S. Air Force*

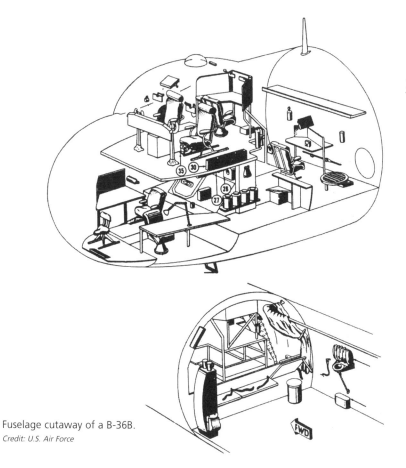

Fuselage cutaway of a B-36B.
Credit: U.S. Air Force

B-36 of the 7th Bomb Wing. *Credit: U.S. Air Force*

Gunner's position in nose.
Credit: U.S. Air Force

Bomb bay interior. *Credit: U.S. Air Force.*

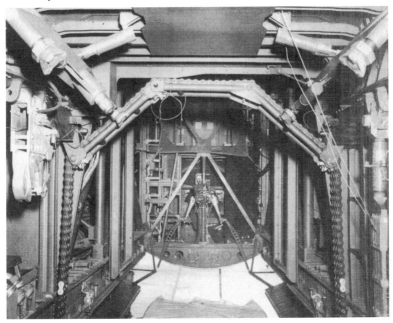

million each. The whole B-36 program cost U.S. taxpayers a staggering $1.4 billion in 1950 dollars, or $14.1 billion today. Although not much in today's dollars, it was the greatest amount ever spent on a military acquisition program to that point.

In the autumn of 1948, the 7th Bomb Wing at Carswell AFB was expected to replace its initial capability B-36A conventional bombers with the nuclear-capable B-36B version. With this conversion, the wing became a service test unit until June 1950. The B-36B that crashed in British Columbia was assigned to the 436th Bombardment Squadron of the 7th Bomb Wing. It was completed on July 31, 1949, and had flown for a total of only 186 hours.

The day after the crash, General Irvine, 7th Bomb Wing Commander, imposed flying restrictions on the B-36s at Carswell, and all flying ground to a halt.

The 7th Bomb Wing's B-36 bomber would become well known in at least one part of Canada, but on the opposite coast from the crash. The wing sent six 492nd Bomb Squadron B-36 bombers to the first-ever deployment to Goose Bay, Newfoundland, Canada, on 17 July 1951. During their stay in Goose Bay, the bombers flew a polar mission and then tested a partial war plan profile attack on Tampa, Florida; Birmingham, Alabama; Fort Worth, Texas; Little Rock, Arkansas; and Dallas, Texas. The second deployment to Canada saw the 436th Bomb Squadron familiarize itself with Goose Bay and test the base facilities for use in staging for atomic attacks on 16 September 1951. The third unit to deploy to Canada was the 9th Bomb Squadron, which on 11 October sent six B-36 bombers to Goose Bay for familiarization.

The last stop for B-36 bombers: the boneyard to await destruction and recycling.
Credit: U.S. Air Force AMARC

Mark-4 Atomic Bomb

Development of the new bomb type began at the Los Alamos laboratory in early 1945 before the end of World War II. In June 1946, the new bomb was named the Mark-4 device.

The Mk-4 was the first mass-produced nuclear weapon in the U.S. arsenal. Over 550 copies of this implosion-type atomic bomb were built. This airdropped weapon could only be detonated in an air burst (above ground level) for maximum destruction of a city. The first bomb entered the arsenal on 19 March 1949; production ended in May 1951 and all were retired to storage and disassembly between July 1952 and May 1953.

The basic concept of the bomb was to provide for a more rugged design with ease of production and increased dependability. The new weapon would also have more user-friendly arming features and could be stored for longer periods than the labor-intensive Fat Man bomb.

The bomb was an improvement of the Fat Man atomic bomb, which had been used against the city of Nagasaki, Japan, in 1945. Its shape was based on an old U.S. Navy design for a C-class World War I blimp. The nuclear bomb components were designed by the Los Alamos Laboratory, and components of the exterior bomb shape were built by American Car & Foundry Company. The assembly of the casing was accomplished by Silas Mason Company in the Iowa Ordnance Plant. With only sixty-one handling and assembly tools and 141 test equipment components, the new bomb was relatively easy to maintain and assemble for use.

During its short service life of less than four years, five bombs were used in nuclear tests and five were lost to accidents. The bulky weapon could be carried to a target city by the B-29, B-47, B-50, AJ-1 and B-36 bombers.

The Mk-4 was the first nuclear weapon to be deployed overseas since World War II, when nine were sent to Anderson Field on Guam during the Korean War in August 1950. The nuclear cores were later sent in April 1951 and plans were made to have the 43rd Bomb Wing drop the bombs on seven Chinese and two Soviet cities in the Far East between Shanghai and Khabarovsk. This is considered the first time custody of a core was transferred from the AEC to the Pentagon, and the nine bombs were the only ones under military control until 1954.

The Mk-4 had a removable core that could be put into or removed from the bomb during flight. A well-trained weaponeer could insert the core and ready the bomb for combat use in less than thirty minutes. But the core was kept separate from the bomb at all times short of war.

To insert the uranium or plutonium core, the weaponeer removed the flat nose plate of the bomb, disconnected the detonator cables, removed two detonators, removed a "polar cap" covering the forward hemisphere of high explosives, removed the outer and then the inner tapered high explosive lenses and pulled out a cylindrical plug made up of the aluminum pusher and the natural uranium tamper. This revealed the space for the core, an eleven-centimeter (4.5-in.) diameter sphere of radioactive materials coated in nickel. The four high-explosive lenses weighed about 156 kilograms (339 lb.); the pusher-tamper 4 kilograms (9 lb.); and the core nearly 6 kilograms (13 lb.). Simple tools were used to insert or extract the core. Less than seven components were removed to make a complete check.

In his 31 July 1998, interview done by Don Pyeatt and posted on the Internet, co-pilot Ray Whitfield recalls, "there were mechanical systems for handling the core, which was not installed for this flight."

In-flight insertion (IFI) and extraction was first attempted with a modified Mk-3 bomb in a parked B-29 bomber on 29 March 1949. The whole extraction and reinsertion took a mere half hour, or one-third the predicted time. The original justification for the test was to see if it was possible to remove the core before an emergency weapon jettison. The Air Force immediately asked the AEC to produce an Mk-4 bomb with IFI features.

In January 1950, the first fifty sets of the H-1 IFI/IFE tools had been built. A lightweight "trap door" assembly was used in conjunction with this equipment. The equipment consisted of a vacuum suction cup on a stick, which attached to the high-explosive lenses that formed the trap door into the core. Lenses, once removed, were stored in baskets beside the weaponeer at the front of the bomb bay. The biggest problem with the vacuum system was that at extreme cold, if frost formed on the lenses, the suction cup would not grasp the surface. Los Alamos then developed a stick with a threaded end that could be screwed into a receptacle on the face of the lens.

Nuclear weapons test "X-Ray" of a Mk-4 bomb.
Credit: U.S. Department of Energy

Different nuclear cores for the Mk-4 were detonated in tests X-ray, Yoke and Zebra of Operation Sandstone in the Marshall Islands. The goal was to produce a larger explosion with less plutonium, a rare and expensive material.

The first test explosion, called X-ray, on 14 April 1948, had a yield of 37 kilotons. X-ray used a composite uranium-plutonium Type B levitated core, which was suspended inside the pit. This meant 2.5 kilograms (5.5 lb.) of plutonium and 5 kilograms (11 lb.) of uranium together in the same sphere. The explosion only released the energy of about 35 percent of the plutonium and around 25 percent of the uranium, so it was not an efficient use of the raw materials. However, the X-ray core produced the largest explosion in the world up to that date.

The second test, Yoke, on 30 April had a yield of 49 kilotons, and the last test, Zebra, on 14 May yielded 18 kilotons. The Zebra device used only highly enriched uranium in the levitated core.

Mk-4 atomic bomb

Length: 3.25 m

Width: 1.54 m

Weight: 4.9 tonnes

Explosive Yield: 20 – 40 kt

Number produced: 550

Years deployed: 1949–1953

Cores:

a. 49-LTC-C levitated uranium-235 Zebra core, 18 kt;

b. 49-LCC-C levitated composite uranium-plutonium X-ray core, 37 kt;

c. 50-LCC-C composite Fox core, 22 kt.

Mk-4 atomic bomb in bare metal finish.
Credit: U.S. Department of Energy

For those interested in the internal workings and dimensions of the Mk-4 atomic bomb, until now there has not been any detail available; however, research done in support of the television documentary about this Broken Arrow yielded the following interesting results.

The original atomic bomb design had thirty-two high-explosive lenses focusing a force inward to the core. The problem is that a sphere cannot be divided into thirty-two identical surface shapes. Luckily, over two thousand years ago Plato discovered that it is possible to interweave a dodecahedron (twelve-sided) with an icosahedron (twenty-sided), and have a nearly regular face on a sphere, like a soccer ball. This is what the twenty hexagonal (six-sided) and twelve pentagonal (five-sided) surfaces are shaped like on the thirty-two outer lens sphere system.

The Mk-4 'pit' package was made up of four distinct components: the nickel-coated core of plutonium and uranium, measuring 11 centimeters (4 in.) across and weighing about 6 kilogram (13 lb.); an air gap 2 centimeters (1 in.) wide surrounding the core; a natural uranium tamper 5 centimeters (2 in.) thick weighing about 50 kilograms (110 lb.); and an aluminum pusher 11 centimeters (4 in.) thick. The aluminum pusher channeled the energy of the inward high explosion toward the core. The uranium tamper, being very dense, both increased the punch of the implosion and held the nuclear reaction in the core for just a moment longer to build up a greater chain reaction. The air gap allowed the inward pressure wave to build up prior to striking the core, just as a hammer is swung at a nail instead of being pushed while sitting on the nail. The core of radioactive material, when compressed, underwent a fission chain reaction and released a tremendous amount of energy.

Surrounding the pit were the dual concentric layers of high explosives that would inwardly compress the pit and, inside it, the core to cause the chain reaction. There were thirty-two inner high explosive (HE) lenses, 21.5 centimeters (8.5 in.) thick and weighing 37 kilograms (82 lb.) each; and thirty-two outer HE lenses, 21.5 centimeters thick and weighing 41 kilograms (90 lb.) each. The lenses were tapered so that they would come to a point in the very center of the sphere in the middle of the core. The total thickness of inner and outer HE lenses was 43 centimeters (16 in.) from the core to the edge, giving the bomb's physics package a diameter of 1.32

meters (4.3 ft.), and the bomb's outer casing an overall diameter of 1.52 meters (4.9 ft.). Total weight of the HE is about 2.5 tonnes (32 x 37 kg + 32 x 41 kg = 2,500 kg or 5,500 lb.).

The core was not installed in the bomb at the factory and was only emplaced in the pit prior to a war mission or test detonation. To get to the center of the pit, which fits snugly inside the sphere of thirty-two inner HE lenses that sit snugly inside another sphere of thirty-two outer HE lenses, there is a trap-door system.

The weaponeer would have to remove the forward-facing polar cap from the metal casing that holds together the physics package. The polar cap allowed access to the outer face of two of the outer HE lenses. By removing two outer lenses and then two inner lenses, weighing approximately 156 kilograms (344 lb.), the weaponeer then had access to the outer edge of the pit. The aluminum pusher, which was about 11 centimeters (4 in.) thick, had a trap door some 12 centimeters (4 in.) across and 11 (4 in.) centimeters thick and weighing about 1 kilogram (2 lb.). Attached to the inside of the pusher was the uranium tamper. The tamper trap door was about 12 centimeters (4 in.) across and 5 centimeters (1.5 in.) thick weighing some 3 kilograms (7 lb.). The trap door through the pit is a regular cylinder straight plug like a coffee can. With these unscrewed from the face of the pit and removed, the 15-centimeter (5-in.) diameter hole at the center of the bomb was now visible to the weaponeer. Once the lenses and plug were removed, the core could be either inserted or extracted through the tiny opening using a vacuum tool on a stick.

Cradle to Grave

In early 1947 the Atomic Energy Commission assumed legal custody of all nuclear weapons, although the AFSWP guarded and maintained the bombs. Only by order of the president could a military organization take custody of the weapon. Although there were already two assembly teams, no one had ever practiced the procedures for turning over a bomb from the AEC to the bombing unit.

The lost Mk-4 bomb had to have come from one of two storage sites in the continental United States. National Stockpile Site (NSS) Able at Manzano base on Kirtland AFB was the first operational storage site, given that it was built for the Manhattan

Project/AFSWP, and was a joint Army/Air Force site. Site Baker at Kileen Base, Fort Hood, Texas, was actually the first designated NSS, becoming operational in 1948. It is located about 18 kilometers east of Gray AFB.

The weapon was moved to Carswell by a transport B-50 bomber prior to being loaded on the B-36 for the flight to Eielson. There was probably both a bomb commander and weaponeer with the bomb at all times.

To protect the secrets of the bomb on this mission, declassified U.S. Air Force secret documents state it was fused for 1,400 meters. The bomb was dropped north-northwest of Princess Royal Island, British Columbia. Crewmen testified they saw it explode 1,100 meters above the water.

"I wanted to get rid of it and blow it because...I could just see a (Russian) sub fishing it off the bottom," said co-pilot Lt. Raymond P. Whitfield Jr.

Captain Barry and his co-pilot Ray Whitfield disagree on what happened when they tried to drop the bomb. According to Barry, "We got out over the water just about 9,000 feet (2,700 m) and the co-pilot ran the bomb bay doors and hit the salvo switch and at first nothing happened, so he hit it again and this time it opened.

However, co-pilot Lt. Raymond P. Whitfield Jr. remembers things this way: "The bomb doors jammed so I ordered the T-handle pulled and the weapon to be dropped through the partially opened bomb doors."

The best evidence suggests that the Mk-4 bomb was dropped out over the Pacific Ocean and detonated above the surface of the water. The detonation destroyed all evidence of the bomb. This was, or at least became, standard operating procedure for SAC when faced with the possible loss of an atomic bomb. We see this procedure repeated in November 1950 with the dropping of an atomic bomb in the St. Lawrence River by a B-50 bomber in distress during a flight from Goose Bay to Tucson, Arizona. The bomb was dropped and detonated, and the crew managed to fly the aircraft to Limestone AFB in Maine.

Evidence from the U.S.A. in the form of documents strongly suggests that the bomb was in fact dropped out of the aircraft prior to it crashing in the mountains. It seems most probable that the bomb was dropped out over the ocean to destroy all evidence.

The bomb shackle at the crash site shows no indication of having held anything at the time of the impact. There are no signs of anything being wrenched out of the shackle upon impact or of something large pushing against the sway braces upon impact. It appears the bomb bay was empty of the Mk-4 bomb when the bomber crashed.

The best explanation is that the Mk-4 bomb was set to detonate at a predetermined altitude, salvoed from the bomb bay and detonated over the Pacific Ocean to destroy all evidence of it and prevent it from falling into the wrong hands.

What an Mk-4 Would Do to a City

The largest yield core deployed in an Mk-4 was the thirty-seven-kiloton X-ray core. Exploded 200 meters (220 yd.) over a city, this atomic bomb would produce a fireball 600 meters (660 yd.) across and a shallow but substantial crater with substantial fallout. The air burst would have to be above 300 meters (330 yd.) altitude to prevent the fireball from touching the ground and, thus, prevent substantial fallout. This bomb is nearly twice the power of the bomb that devastated the city of Nagasaki, Japan, killing tens of thousands in a few seconds.

The 37-kt blast would level reinforced concrete structure 900 meters (990 yd.) from Ground Zero (GZ); it would collapse most factories and commercial buildings and destroy small wood-frame and brick houses 1.5 kilometers (0.95 mi.) from GZ. It would destroy lightly constructed commercial buildings and typical residences and inflict serious damage to heavier construction 2 kilometers (1.25 mi.) from GZ. The walls of typical steel-frame buildings would be

Nagasaki mushroom cloud, 09 August 1945.
Credit: U.S. Department of Energy

blown away, and cause severe damage to residences, with winds sufficient to kill people out in the open 2.7 kilometers (1.7 mi.) from GZ. There would be lighter damage to structures and people would be endangered by flying glass and debris 6 kilometers from GZ.

The largest yield ever attained by an Mk-4 in a test, though this was never fielded, was forty-nine kilotons. An explosion of a forty-nine-kiloton atomic bomb in airburst mode at 200 meters (220 yd.) altitude over a city would produce a shallow crater and substantial fallout.

The blast would level reinforced concrete structure one kilometer (0.6 mi.) from Ground Zero; collapse most factories and commercial buildings, and destroy small wood-frame and brick houses 1.6 kilometers (1 mi.) from GZ. It would destroy lightly constructed commercial buildings and typical residences and inflict serious damage to heavier construction 2.3 kilometers (1.4 mi.) from GZ. The walls of typical steel-frame buildings would be blown away and cause severe damage to residences, with winds sufficient to kill people out in the open 3 kilometers (2 mi.) from GZ. There would be lighter damage to structures, and people endangered by flying glass and debris 6 kilometers (4 mi.) from GZ.

In short, even this small weapon would destroy the core of a medium-sized city.

Chapter 2: Seventeen Men and the Mission to Bomb San Francisco

Entire crew lined up at the nose of the aircraft prior to a flight. *Credit: U.S. Air Force*

The Mission

Based at Carswell Air Force Base, Fort Worth, Texas, the crew of bomber #44-92075 was going to the coldest place imaginable in preparation for their unusual training mission. SAC had directed the 7th Bomb Wing to send several aircraft to Eielson AFB, Alaska, as part of a practice strike force utilizing atomic weapons to attack a target inside the United States. The flight would help develop procedures for working with atomic weapons from forward operating locations, especially in the far north.

Following is the documented notification of a briefing given to combat crew:

Briefing of Aircraft Crew (Secret)

The formal briefing for the combat crews on B-36 AF No. 44-92075 was conducted at Carswell AFB, 1 Feb. 50. Specialized briefings were conducted after the formal briefing for pilots, observers, flight engineers, radio operators and gunners. The strike crews were then transported to Eielson AFB on C-54 aircraft to await the arrival of B-36 aircraft for the strike mission over San Francisco. At 0830 AST, 13 Feb. 50, a final briefing was conducted at EAFB for Capt. Barry and Capt. Cooper's crews. This briefing covered operations, flight engineering, and weather. Specialized briefings were held for pilots, observers, flight engineers, radio operators, bomb commanders and weaponeers. These specialized briefings covered all changes to the original plan and stressed emergency procedures for bad icing conditions which could be encountered enroute to ZI. The weather officers and the undersigned instructed the crews to change their flight plan to be above the clouds if serious icing was encountered enroute from Anchorage to Cape Flattery. Radio operators were briefed on reporting procedures and communications problems peculiar to this mission especially while out of the ZI. The flight engineers were given data on cold weather starting and operations peculiar to the Alaskan area.

Lt. Col. George T. Chadwell,
USAF, S-3, 7th Strike Group

Crew being inspected at the nose of the aircraft prior to a flight. *Credit: U.S. Air Force*

Their combat-profile training mission called on the crew to fly from Eielson AFB, Alaska, along the coast of British Columbia, then through the continental United States on a bombing mission aimed at San Francisco. This training mission simulated the profile of an actual combat mission, including night and high-altitude flying. After one or more practice bombing runs, they would fly directly to their home base.

The flight plan was "120 R39 B26 A1 Cape Flattery 140 Drct Fort Peck 400 Solonsea Drct Frisco 400 Drct to destination Fort Worth."

Flight Plan

Five-segment path:		8,672 km
64°42'00" N, 147°06'00" W,	48°20'00" N, 124°40'00" W	2,260 km
48°20'00" N, 124°40'00" W,	42S (48°06'57" N, 105°10'56" W)	1,444 km
42S (48°06'57" N, 105°10'56"W)	SAS (33°14'29" N, 115°57'09" W)	1,882 km
SAS (33°14'29" N, 115°57'09" W)	SFO (37°37'08" N, 122°22'30" W)	759 km
SFO (37°37'08" N, 122°22'30" W)	32°46'00" N, 97°26'00" W	2,327 km

The bomber was ferried to Alaska by a secondary crew, while the primary crew had been flown in from Carswell earlier that day in a C-54 transport aircraft.

But 44-92075 was not alone on the mission. It was joined by 44-92083 of the same squadron, and also armed with a real Mk-4 atomic bomb. Both bombs had been picked up and flown in two B-50 bombers to Carswell AFB where each was loaded into one of the two new giant bombers for the flight to Eielson AFB. The bomb had to be brought in to Carswell initially, as at the time the U.S. Air Force did not have custody of nuclear weapons: they were held by the Atomic Energy Commission. The target city of 44-92083 remains unknown, but also could well have been San Francisco.

The weather at Eielson was so cold that de-icing was almost impossible. Crews kept the engines running at all times to provide heat for de-icing the wings. Lt. Whitfield recalled that if the engines stopped, the oil would solidify. Canadian bush pilots in the north used to actually light fires underneath engines in order to thaw them. Later, a safer stove was developed; it blew heat rather than flames directly on to the engine.

Ominously, Captain Harold Barry had never flown in the Arctic prior to this mission. The flight left Eielson at 4:27 p.m. and headed south. It was a twenty-four-hour flight, and the aircraft had twen-

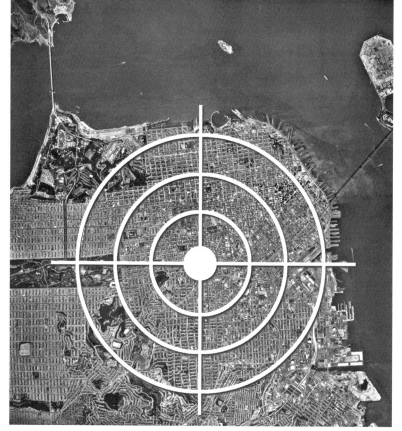

Aerial photo of central San Francisco. *Credit: U.S. Navy*

ty-eight hours worth of fuel and one atomic bomb. After more than sixteen hours of flight, the crew would conduct the full-simulated bomb run against the city of San Francisco. They would test all wartime operations except actually dropping their real bomb.

San Francisco was an ideal target for practice bombing runs. As the center of the city is on a giant peninsula surrounded on three sides by water, it would show up clearly on radar bomb screens. Landmarks such a bridges and islands were easily identified. It was also on the coast, so that in the event of an emergency, the bomber could be ditched at sea. The fact that it was the U.S. stand-in for the Russian city of Leningrad explains why SAC commander General LeMay wrote in his autobiography that "San Francisco had been bombed over 600 times in a month" during SAC's rehearsal for nuclear combat against Russia.

In his 31 July 1998 interview done by Don Pyeatt and posted on

Crewmen Ray Whitfield and his wife and Paul Gerhart and his wife on their return to Texas after the incident. *Credit: Fort Worth Star-Telegram*

the Internet, co-pilot Ray Whitfield recalls the flight prior to the accident. "Most of the time was spent climbing toward our 40,000 feet cruising altitude. We were very heavy with the full combat configuration and our top speed was less than 200 knots during the climb. I was acting as co-pilot for Capt. Barry. I volunteered to go on the flight as one of the co-pilots since the aircraft was permanently assigned to me. I wanted to be on the flight to be able to look after my plane."

The Crew

Survivors

Lt. Colonel Daniel V. MacDonald (probably the AFSWP Bomb Commander)

Captain Harold L. Barry, 29 (aircraft commander)

Lt. Ernest O. Cox, 28 (engineer)

Lt. Ray R. Darrah, age unknown (observer)

Lt. Paul E. Gerhart, 26 (radar operator)

Lt. Raymond P. Whitfield Jr., 23 (co-pilot)

Lt. C.G. Pooler, 36 (engineer)

T/Sgt. Martin B. Stephens, 30 (gunner)

S/Sgt. James R. Ford, 28 (gunner)

S/Sgt. Dick Thrasher, 29 (gunner)

S/Sgt. Vitale Trippodi, age unknown (gunner)

Cpl. Richard J. Schuler, 23 (radio mechanic)

Cox and Barry greeted by their wives.
Credit: *Forth Worth* Star-Telegram

Captain Harold Barry greeted by his wife
on his return to Texas after the incident.
Credit: *Forth Worth* Star-Telegram

The accident took a horrible toll on the men; within months, many had gone back to civilian life, among them the co-pilot Ray Whitfield.

Captain Harold L. Barry, the aircraft commander and pilot was only twenty-nine years old at the time of the accident. He was called back to active duty from the U.S. Air Force Reserve due to a pilot shortage. Barry had learned to fly in World War II, and got his wings on July 28, 1943. He had a lot of experience with the B-36, with 900 hours as the first pilot and 577 hours as the co-pilot or student. He had also put in 168 hours as the pilot of the B-36B type aircraft, with another fifty as co-pilot or student.

Both Captain Barry and S/Sgt. Thrasher remained in the air force and even flew together. A year later they were scheduled for another training mission closer to Carswell. Following are comments from S/Sgt. Dick Thrasher regarding the prospects of their next mission.

"Barry said, 'Is Thrasher going with us.' Well I answered 'Yes, Thrasher is going. This is his crew. When they fly he flies.' Barry said, 'We're bound to have trouble.' That's the last words I heard out of Barry. It seemed like there was something wrong with Barry and I flying together because we always had trouble."

Barry and the other flight deck crew were killed when their cockpit was destroyed in flight by an Oklahoma Air National Guard

P-51 Mustang crashing through the canopy. Thrasher, in the rear compartment, parachuted to safety from a second B-36 disaster.

Missing

Captain William M. Phillips, 30 (navigator)
Captain Theodore F. Schreier, 35 (AFSWP Weaponeer)
Lt. Holiel Ascol, 37 (bombardier)
S/Sgt Elbert W. Pollard, 28 (gunner)
S/Sgt Neil A. Straley, 30 (gunner)

Holiel Ascol, born in Sioux City, Iowa, was a combat pilot in World War II. He flew fifty-three missions in the far north Pacific and was awarded the Purple Heart and Air Medal.

Those missing are presumed to have drowned in the icy waters of the north Pacific Ocean between Ashdown Island and Princess Royal Island. This is evidenced by the fact that a one-man dinghy was washed up on a shore in this area.

These crew members were never found, with the exception of a foot in a boot recovered by a fisherman near Princess Royal Island later that year. The bones of the foot are buried in a grave marked with the names of all the missing men. It was standard practice of the U.S. military during the Korean War-era to dust all bodies with a white powder acting as a desiccant before burial.

With the discovery of DNA and advances in DNA technology, decades later the U.S. military had hopes of identifying the bones. In 2002 the remains were exhumed and sent to the Central Identification Laboratory of the Joint POW/MIA Accounting Command in Hawaii. But there was no DNA to be found in the bones. It turns out that the white powder used by the military fifty years ago had the effect of stripping DNA from remains, so that even well-preserved bodies have no genetic markers. The bones remain unidentified but are still presumed to belong to one of the missing five men.

Weaponeers and Bomb Commanders

In early 1946 General Leslie Groves, the head of the wartime Manhattan Project to build the atomic bomb, agreed to train six Army-Air Force colonels and five junior officers as atomic weaponeers. Army-Air Force General Ramey told LeMay on March 29, 1946, that "those duties are not nearly so complicated as we have been told. As a matter of fact, I have made some little study of them myself and believe, in a pinch, I could tell whether the bomb was ready to go."

There were two special crew members associated with delivering the bomb: the bomb commander and the weaponeer. The weaponeer armed the bomb, and the bomb commander supervised the weaponeer and certified the bomb as ready. The commander was a colonel responsible for coordinating bomb assembly and delivering the bomb at the loading site. As Lt. Colonel MacDonald was not a regular crewmember, his high rank could denote he was the bomb commander given temporary custody of the Mk-4 lost on this training mission.

In the autumn of 1946 the Manhattan Project was dissolved, and the Pentagon gained control of the new Armed Forces Special Weapons Project (AFSWP), of which Groves was now the commander. His deputy was Rear-Admiral William Parsons, the first atomic weaponeer, and a U.S. Navy man. The bomb had always been an army-navy item, with the air force called in only to deliver the package at the end of the project.

The operational concept called for bomb commanders to be colonels assigned to atomic units or key staff positions following a short course from the scientific staff who built the bombs. Weaponeers would be more junior and receive longer more specialized training with the AFSWP. Groves established the 2761st Engineering Battalion (Special) at Sandia Base, New Mexico, and brought in twenty-seven young engineering officers to be weaponeers. The battalion would also assemble bombs. The AAF insisted the weaponeers be air officers and full crew members.

By the end of 1946, thirty air officers were being trained as bomb commanders in a three-week instructional course. The weaponeer course was twenty-four weeks long and the first one was to produce forty-five AAF weaponeer officers. The initial batch of courses were to run through 1947.

Groves concluded there would be no need for further training after the first batch had been certified. The air staff felt it needed 200 weaponeers and 180 bomb commanders just to begin to meet their future force projections. Groves did not listen and canceled the bomb commanders course in 1947 stating that the original quota, twenty, had been met. SAC Commander LeMay demanded another 114 bomb commanders, and Groves said to train that number would endanger information security. This was resolved in favor of SAC, but the training of weaponeers soon fell far behind as a result of the difficulty in finding highly qualified aircrews.

At the beginning of 1948 only six crews were qualified to drop the bomb, although there were personnel available to make up another fourteen emergency crews. Atomic units had a nearly 100 percent personnel turnover the previous year because of recruiting and retention problems. The most serious problem was a lack of weaponeers. By the end of September 1948, seventy crews were ready and more bomb commanders and weaponeers were expected. A fourth assembly team was forming. Eighteen months later, SAC had eighteen atomic assembly teams.

Captain Schreier, Weaponeer

After World War II, Theodore (Ted) Schreier left the Army Air Force for civilian life. By 1946 the airline industry was beginning to boom, Ted started work with the growing American Airlines. Postwar life seemed good as he and his wife Jean began civilian life in Madison, Wisconsin. But only a year later Ted was recalled to active duty with the air force, which by then was suffering a nation-wide manpower shortage.

Ted Schreier's pilot certificate from American Airlines.
Photos courtesy of Diefenbunker, Canada's Cold War Museum Collection

Weaponeer Captain
Theodore Schreier.

Left to right: Ted in a casual moment; Jean Schreier; Jean and Ted with their nephew. *Photos courtesy of Diefenbunker, Canada's Cold War Museum Collection*

After requalifying for air force wings, Schreier was selected to attend the training given by the Armed Forces Special Weapons Project. He became one of the tiny cadre of weaponeers, and was responsible for arming a Mk-4 atomic weapon. So secret was his job that Schreier's diary entry for the day he became part of the nuclear weapons staff is only a cryptic "AFSWP." From then on, his diary is almost devoid of comment.

It seems that the U.S. Air Force had originally told Schreier's family he was the pilot of a transport plane. "We were never told any details about the mission, what it entailed, we found out later he was the third pilot and the weaponeer," said his nephew Fred Schreier.

In his July 1998 Internet interview with Don Pyeatt, co-pilot Ray Whitfield recalls that he "pointed out to Schreier that he had his floatation vest on over his parachute. At this time he and Barry and I were the last ones on the plane. Schreier was hurriedly removing his vest when Barry ordered me out. Barry exited after me. I never saw Schreier jump, and he is one of the missing men. No one knows if he did or did not jump except Barry, and he is now deceased."

There are two theories about his death. The first is that he died from hypothermia or drowning when he landed in the freezing waters near Gil Island. The second is that he stayed with the aircraft and flew it towards the crash site.

"No one seen him bail out, no one could testify that they seen him bail out," said S/Sgt. Dick Thrasher.

Even stranger, the U.S. Air Force named streets after the other four missing crew members, but not after Schreier. Some suppose this is due to the fact they wished the involvement of a weaponeer covered-up, but as his being part of the crew on the failed flight was well known to everyone who could read a newspaper, there is likely another reason.

As one of only a handful of weaponeers in the entire world, he was not a regular crewmember, but could be assigned to any bomber carrying a nuclear weapon. He was not part of the aircrew assigned to bomber 92075, nor was he of high rank, and therefore not considered worthy of a street memorial.

We do not know what happened to Capt. Schreier. The most likely scenario is that he was the last to bail out of the aircraft and that by the time he got out, the bomber was already once again over water. Therefore he probably perished within minutes of hitting the very cold ocean.

There is a slim possibility that Schreier did not bail out of the aircraft with the other sixteen crewmen. It is possible that he stayed with the bomber and flew it to the crash site in the mountains. If he died in the crash or of exposure in the aftermath, then it would explain reports of a body being taken out of the crash site in 1954. However, the fact that he was not a B-36 pilot and that the massive B-36 required several flight crew, mitigates against his having flown the aircraft by himself for so long as to reach the crash site.

My personal belief, based on the probable fact that the bomb had already been dropped and that there was no reason to stay aboard a plummeting aircraft, is that Capt. Schreier bailed out too late, missed land and drowned or froze in the Pacific Ocean. Without the bodies, it may never be known what happened to Theodore Schreier or the four other missing crew members.

Chapter 3: Everything Goes Wrong

There was bad weather along the Alaska and B.C. coastline, but it should have been manageable by the giant bomber. The cloud ceiling ranged from a high of 700 meters (770 yd.) to a low of 150 meters (165 yd.), being broken or solid overcast throughout the area. Visibility ranged from five to twenty kilometers, and there was a light rain. The winds were from the southeast and east-southeast, ranging from 30 km/h (15 mph) to as high as 80 km/h (50 mph).

The weather in the Port Hardy area at the time of the incident was overcast with a ceiling of 640 meters (2,100 ft.) and lower broken clouds. The wind was ESE at 29 km/h (18 mph), with a visibility of 19 kilometers (12 mi.) in light rain. Cape St. James was experiencing light rain with an overcast at 150 meters (500 ft.). The wind was southeast at 83 km/h (52 mph) with a visibility of 5 kilometers (3 mi.).

Icing conditions were scattered throughout the flight path, but this fact was unknown to the pilot. Captain Barry told the accident board of inquiry that, "I hadn't flown in the Arctic and I didn't know when you are liable to get iced up there. I figured that as cold as it is was all the moisture in the air should already be frozen."

The aircraft began to build up ice on the wings, tail, engines and propellers and then started to lose altitude. The airplane struggled to stay aloft, and the crew applied more power. Engine #1 caught fire and was immediately shut down. Just before midnight, the crew sent their first emergency broadcast from the stricken aircraft, and the bomber almost immediately began to lose altitude. Power was reduced on the other engines, but #2 and #5 caught fire within minutes and were also shut down. Emergency power was applied on the remaining three engines, but the aircraft was dropping toward the sea at about 30 meters (33 yd.) per minute.

Southam news reporter David Pugliese writes that several aircraft sent many messages that night. Another B-36 flying the same

Members of the official U.S. Air Force board of inquiry meeting at Carswell Air Force Base on 18 February 1950 to determine the cause of the crash. They were not cleared to discuss the loss of the atomic bomb. *Credit: U.S. Air Force*

route is said to have heard the distress call and forwarded the message to the United States. He also notes in his 13 February 2000 article that a Langley Airways crew heard, "B-36 mayday, water landing between Queen Charlotte Island Sound and Vancouver Island." None of the message traffic is verifiable today.

Dirk Septer, in his *BC Aviator* magazine article from 1993, wrote that the first message, transmitted at 23:25, stated the aircraft was in difficulty at 40,000 feet. He also reports a second transmission as saying, "One engine on fire. Contemplate ditching in Queen Charlotte Sound between Queen Charlotte Island and Vancouver Island. Keep a careful lookout for flares or wreckage."

Captain Barry described the final minutes of the flight to General Atkinson of the official U.S. Air Force Board of Inquiry:

That was the maximum [speed] and just about that time we had a fire in #1. About the time we leveled off – 15,000 feet [4,600 m], and that was in #1. As soon as the scanner called in – fire in #1 coming out around the airplug, the engineer feathered it and turned the manual switch to stop it. The scanner called fire in #2, so he feathered that one and between the fire in #1 and 2 the engineers changed seats, the 2nd engineer asked the scanner where the fire was coming from – and he said from the top of the air plug, so he was about to get things settled down when the right scanner called fire in #5, so he feathered that one, and by that time we were losing altitude quite rapidly in excess of 500 feet a minute [150 m/min.] and I asked the Radar Operator to give me a heading to take me out over water. We kept our rapid rate of descent and we got out over the water just about 9000 feet [2,700 m] and the co-pilot hit the salvo switch. The Radar Operator gave me a heading to take me back over land, the engineer gave me emergency power to try to hold our altitude. We still descended quite rapidly and by the time we got over land we were at 5000 feet [1,500 m]. So, I rang the alarm bell, and told them to leave. The Radar Operator told me that there was terrain which in a few places ran up to 3500 feet [1,000 meters] and that is one reason I wanted them out.

S/Sgt. Dick Thrasher said, "The next thing I remember was Barry, and he told us to get ready to bail out. But, he says first we have to go out over the water and get rid of this weapon."

At the rate it was losing altitude, it should have crashed in less than ten minutes. The bomber, without bomb and presumably without crew, mysteriously proceeded to a site 350 km away from the bailout point and crashed near Mount Kologet in the Kispiox Valley at 56°03'00" N, 128°32'00" W.

Instead of heading out to sea, it turned 180 degrees to fly north, gained at least 800 meters (880 yd.) altitude and climbed over several mountain ranges and flew for at least two more hours to reach the crash site. Unverified oral histories of the incident include eye-

WAR DEPARTMENT
AAF Form No. 14
Rev. 1 Oct. '44

~~SECRET~~

ARMY AIR FORCES

REPORT OF MAJOR ACCIDENT

Use this form in accordance with AAF Reg. 62-14 and "Aircraft Accident Investigator's Handbook" issued by Office of Flying Safety, Headquarters, AAF.

Fill in all spaces except where otherwise indicated.

If additional space is needed, use additional sheet(s) and identify by proper section letter and subsection number.

Section A—GENERAL INFORMATION

1. PLACE OF ACCIDENT—State, County, Nearest Town, Distance and Direction from Same. Nearest Army Airport, Distance and Direction from Same.
Princess Royal Island, British Columbia, Canada   180 sm - 330° McChord AFB, Tacoma, Washington

2. WAS COLLISION WITH OTHER AIRCRAFT? ☐ Yes ☒ No   AF No. of AIRCRAFT INVOLVED (File separate Form 14 for each aircraft) 44-92075   DATE 14 Feb 50   HOUR and TIME ZONE 0:05Z   ☐ DAY ☐ NIGHT

Section B—AIRCRAFT

1. AIRCRAFT NO.	2. TYPE	MODEL	SERIES	3. HOME STATION
44-92075	B	36	B	Carswell Air Force Base, Fort Worth, Texas

4. AIR FORCE OR COMMAND	SUBCOMMAND	WING	GROUP NO. AND TYPE	SQUADRON
SAC	8th AF	7th Bomb Wing	7th Bomb Group (H)	436th

5. DATE OF MANUFAC.	TOTAL HOURS	DATE LAST OVERHAUL	OVERHAULING DEPOT OR NON-DEPOT	HOURS SINCE OVERHAUL
July 49	185:25	New	New	New

Section C—OPERATOR (Person at controls at time of accident)

1. LAST NAME	FIRST NAME	MIDDLE INITIAL	GRADE	BRANCH	ASN	SEX	AGE
BARRY	HAROLD	L.	Captain	USAFR	AO308241	M	29

2. ATTACHED STATION	AF OR COMMAND	SUBCOMMAND	WING	GROUP NO. AND TYPE	SQUADRON
Same as 3 below					

3. ASSIGNED STATION	AF OR COMMAND	SUBCOMMAND	WING	GROUP NO. AND TYPE	SQUADRON
Carswell AFB	SAC	8th AF	7th BW	7th BG (H)	436th

4. AERONAUTICAL RATING? ☒ Yes ☐ No   PRESENT RATING Pilot   DATE RECEIVED 28 Jul 43   5. NORMAL DUTY STATUS Airplane Commander

Section D—OPERATOR'S FLYING EXPERIENCE (Including civilian)

FLYING TIME	1ST PILOT OR SOLO STUDENT	OTHER PILOT OR OTHER STUDENT		
1. TOTAL HOURS	1403:00	1262:00		
2. HOURS THIS TYPE	900:00	577:00		
3. HOURS THIS MODEL	162:00	50:00		
4. HOURS LAST 90 DAYS	42:00	11:00		
5. HOURS LAST 30 DAYS	34:00	10:00		
6. HOURS LAST 24 HOURS	07:25	00:00		
7. ACTUAL COMBAT HOURS	00:00	304:00		

Fill in items 8 and 9 only if operator was student in training or rated pilot in CIS, OTU, etc.

8. TRAINEE CLASS NO. and SCHOOL, OTU, CCTS, ETC.

9. PHASE AND HOURS IN THIS PHASE

PHASE	DUAL OR COPILOT	SOLO OR 1ST PILOT

10. AAF SCHOOLS PREVIOUSLY ATTENDED AND DATES
Primary Flying Sch   Feb 1943
Basic Flying Sch   to
Advance Flying Sch   Aug 1943
B-17 Transition-Aut to Oct 43

11. INSTRUMENT RATING
TYPE Green   DATE 13 May 50
LAST CHECK STATION CAFB   DATE 16 Jan 50

12. Was operator on instruments at time of accident or immediately before? ☒ Yes ☐ No

If answer to number 12 is Yes, or if accident occurred at night or under instrument or contact conditions, fill in items 13 through 17.

	1ST PILOT	OTHER PILOT
13. TOTAL—INSTRUMENT	221	57
14. INSTRUMENT LAST 6 MOS.	31	6
15. INSTRUMENT LAST 30 DAYS	16	4
16. NIGHT, LAST 6 MOS.	15	4
17. NIGHT, LAST 30 DAYS	3	3

Section E—PERSONNEL INVOLVED (Including operator and all other persons, whether in plane or not)

DUTY AT ACCIDENT	NAME (Last Name First)	TYPE OF AERO. RATING	SERIAL No.	GRADE AND BRANCH OF SERVICE	PERS. CLASS SYMBOL (AAF Reg. 15-1)	ORG. ASSIGNMENT—AIR FORCE OR COMMAND GROUP NUMBER AND TYPE STATION	FATAL MAJOR MINOR NONE MISSING UNKNOWN	PARACHUTE USED	NECESSARY FOR
		(3)		(5)		(7)	(8)	(9)(10)	(11)(12)
AC	BARRY, HAROLD L.		AO308241	Capt USAFR		SAC, 8th AF 7th Bomb Wing 7th Bomb Gp (H) 436th Bomb Sq Carswell AFB			
X									

See attachment number 1   (84)   RESTRICTED

Report of a Major Accident, 14 February 1950.

Declassified and released by the U.S. Air Force under Freedom of Information

witness accounts from people who claim to have seen the aircraft flying over Vancouver Island, burning and making noise.

Instead of flying a mission of nearly 9,000 kilometers (5,500 mi.), the bomber flew about 2,000 kilometers (1,225 mi.) to crash on Mt. Kologet. The initial manned flight from Eielson to the bailout point at 53°02'00" N, 129°10'30" W is about 1,650 kilometers (1,005 mi.). A direct line from there to the crash site at 56°03'00" N, 128°32'00" W is another 340 kilometers (210 mi.).

The U.S. Air Force accident Board of Inquiry convened at Carswell AFB concluded that the aircraft iced up and that this limited their climb ability even with full climbing power. Then, fires developed in three engines, and although emergency power was applied to the remaining three engines, the bomber could not maintain level flight. The board noted that at approximately 5,000 feet (1,500 m) "the crew executed a successful bailout of all crew members."

The records of the crewmen would not be tarnished by the crash. The board ruled that the crew was competent and that "the accident did not occur as a result of any incompetence or lack of good judgment on the part of any crew member."

Chapter 4: Bailout!

The aircraft flew over mountainous Princess Royal Island where U.S. military records report all seventeen men bailed out from 1,500 meters (1,650 yd.) into the cold, dark rain. It was five minutes past midnight on 14 February.

Captain Barry told the press that his aircraft "dropped to 5,000 feet [from 15,000 ft.] in ten minutes." He continued, "Only myself and Lt. Ray Whitfield knew we were really in trouble." Barry said that when he asked the radar operator for a fix on the nearest land, it was a mere three miles away. "When we got near land we were rapidly losing altitude so I put the plane in a slow turn, put it on the automatic pilot and got in line to bail out." Barry asserts that, "I was the last one out of the front compartment."

Survivors of B-36 stated course was being plotted from radar screen steering 030 degrees magnetic as radioed when over Estevan Island 2345P. When in the vicinity of Whale Channel they altered course to 165 degrees magnetic. When three miles [5 km] inland the order to jump was given and all were out in ten seconds. Possibility that six missing men are to the north of where survivors landed on Princess Royal Island, Gil Island, or Whale Channel.

RCAF Search & Rescue Report, Operation Brix, February 1950.

They were ill-prepared for a jump into the Canadian north. The entire crew wore regular winter dry suits, which allowed for air circulation. They were supposed to have changed into wet suits for the overwater part of the flight but had not done so, apparently for reasons of comfort. This was a mistake that probably killed five men and injured others.

The heading of the B-36 at the time of bail-out was 165 degrees true. The first man jumped at point 53.12N by 128.57W. First

WEATHER: Showers today and Wednesday, continuous rain tonight. Low tonight 40; high Wednesday 48.

SHOWERS

The Vancouver Sun

TODAY'S TIDES: High 5:33 a.m. 15.0 feet; low 10:46 a.m. 11.4 feet; high 2:43 p.m. 12.5 feet; low 10:31 p.m. 1.8 feet.

FOUNDED 1886 VOL. LXIV—No. 113 MArine 1161 28 PAGES VANCOUVER, [illegible] COLUMBIA, TUESDAY, FEBRUARY 14, 1950 FINAL ★★★

DESERTED HUBBY LEAPS SIX FLOORS TO DEATH

SAN FRANCISCO, Feb. 14 — (AP) — A man leaped to death from a sixth-floor window, into crowded Market Street today.

With the eyes of hundreds on him, the young man threw his hat to the sidewalk and gestured with his arms for the crowd to clear a space. Then he jumped. Police identified him as Edmond Lewis, 35, of San Francisco, a machinist, whose wife left him Wednesday, taking their two small children.

Churchill Urges Talk With Stalin on Bomb

Indicates He Will Make New Bid To End Cold War If Elected

By British United Press

EDINBURGH, Scotland, Feb. 14.—Winston Churchill called tonight for "another talk" with Soviet Premier Joseph Stalin in a supreme attempt to end the East-West atomic arms race and the cold war.

The Conservative leader in effect promised that if his party wins the February 23 general election, he as prime minister will seek another meeting with Russia "upon the highest level."

Churchill make his proposal at a packed rally in Usher Hall.

Both Laborite Prime Minister Clement R. Attlee, for Britain, and Secretary of State Dean Acheson, for the United States, have rejected proposals for a Big Three or Big Four conference with Stalin in recent weeks.

STALIN WILLING

The official Anglo-American attitude has been that a meeting would be useless unless Russia shows some sign of willingness to compromise its previous adamant stand on such controversial issues as international control of atomic energy and a German peace treaty.

However Moscow dispatches have indicated that Stalin would be willing to participate in a conference.

Churchill bitterly criticized the Labor government for having failed to make the atom bomb itself. He said it was "one of the most extraordinary administrative lapses that have ever taken place."

The Soviet world has by far the greatest military force in the world, the Conservative Party leader said, but the United States has the atom bomb.

"And now, we are told, they have a thousandfold more terrible manifestation of this awful power."

'CHINA NOT LOST'

Churchill read off a list of nations which have fallen into the hands of "the immensely powerful band of men gathered together in the Kremlin."

When he came to China, he added:

"But I do not regard China as having finally accepted Soviet servitude."

Churchill drew mingled cheers and boos this morning when he arrived in Edinburgh in an effort to carry Scotland's 71 seats in the House of Commons.

The boos were the first of the campaign directed against Churchill.

"Down with the Tories," some workmen shouted, but they were drowned out by cheers from Conservative supporters.

Teachers' Wage Bid Rejected

A three-man arbitration board in a majority decision today rejected demands of Vancouver men senior high school teachers for a wage increase.

For the second year in a row, male teachers have been turned down by a board. They were asking a minimum of $2700 a year and a maximum of $5000.

Present minimum for a male teacher with a BA degree is $2100. A teacher with an MA degree can earn as high as $4500.

In a report signed by J. G. Sinclair, chairman, and school board nominee J. D. Ross, the board said "we are not convinced that there is any special factor involved in the position of senior high school teachers compared to those of other groups which is not taken into consideration in the present schedule."

Teachers' nominee, G. S. Ford, dissented.

Meanwhile, arbitration boards sitting in North and West Vancouver have granted wage increases that will give teachers boosts ranging from $100 to $185 a year.

The wage boosts affect all teachers in the North Shore school system.

Greetings Received From Jewish State

By Sun Staff Reporter

VICTORIA, Feb. 14. — Greetings to British Columbia from the new State of Israel were read by Madam Speaker Hodges at the opening of the Legislature today.

They came from Joseph Sprinzak, Speaker of the Knesset, Israel's Parliament, and were conveyed to B.C. in a letter carried by Opposition Leader Harold Winch, and addressed to the Speaker. Mr. Winch had a two-hour talk with Mr. Sprinzak when he visited Europe and the Near East last summer.

CANBERRA, Australia, Feb. 14 —(BUP)—Prime Minister Robert Gordon Menzies announced today that the King and Queen have postponed their proposed visit to Australia until 1952 at the earliest.

LONDON, Feb. 14—(BUP)—Queen Mother Mary, recovering from an attack of sciatica, was decidedly better today, her doctors reported.

Mather's Nightcap

By BARRY MATHER

"What, asked Jones, coming out of the den, "is that thing you got pinned on the wall in there?"

"It's Beverley's painting," his wife said. "Isn't it TERRIFIC? She did it in Art Expression period."

"Art Expression," Jones repeated. "In Grade Three they have Art Expression . . . What's it supposed to be?"

"Well," Mrs. Jones said, "it isn't important what it's supposed to be. The thing is the children express themselves in color . . . it's good for them."

"I'm glad to hear it," Jones said. "I thought at first, it was supposed to be something."

"Didn't you see what she's called it?" his wife asked. "You go and look at it and see the title she gave it."

WHAT'S IN A NAME?

"She calls it 'Design'," Jones said, coming back from looking.

"It's really wonderful the way they encourage children to express their feelings like that," Mrs. Jones remarked.

"Yeh," Jones said. "I guess so. I see she spells Design—D-e-s-i-n-e. I know what it's supposed to be though."

"What?" his wife asked.

"A circus," Jones said. "It's a picture of a circus with a bunch of tents at the back and a merry-go-round in the front . . . What're you laughing at?"

"Oh!" Mrs. Jones said. "A circus! Don't tell her you thought it was a circus. It's a design made up by using straight and curved lines. It's mountain peaks and a lake," she said.

"Mountains and a lake?" Jones repeated. "How do you know?" he asked.

CRITICS AT WORK

"I asked her to EXPLAIN it to me," his wife said. "I asked her in a way that wouldn't impair her confidence in herself or anything. She said it was mountain peaks and a lake."

"'Impair her confidence'," Jone said. "You using words like that, now. Big talk," he said.

He went back to the den for another look.

"If they're mountains how come she made the tops CLEAR and the snow DOWN on the mountains? You ever see mountains like that?"

"Well," Mrs. Jones said, "who cares about that? After all she's only eight."

"Listen," Jones said — "why put a thing like that in the den? It sure looks like . . . it looks pretty cheap to have a thing like that on the wall there."

"Oh," his wife exclaimed. "She was SO proud of it . . . so PLEASED when I put it there . . ."

ANYWHERE ELSE

"Put it in the basement," Jones said. "Put it in her room . . . but not in the den. I mean, after all . . . Hey!" he cried, "Now wait a minute—you don't need to get mad like that . . . you don't have to . . ."

But his wife, suddenly whisked their daughter's art from the wall, marched by him in cold dignity.

"Put it in the kitchen," Jones offered. "Listen—put it in the kitchen . . ."

An hour later Mrs. Jones, entering the den, surprised her husband in the act of tacking their daughter's painting back on the wall.

"We can take it down tomorrow," she said.

"Oh well," Jones said.

A GOOD EVENING to everybody, especially all art students.

Plane[illegible]oats Seek U.S. Bomber Dow[illegible] With 17 Men Off B.C.

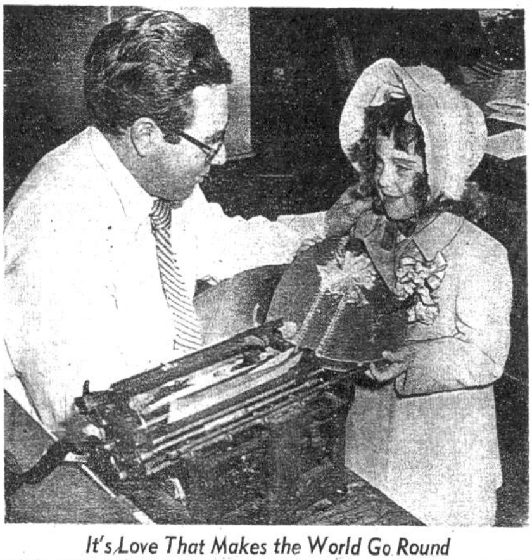

It's Love That Makes the World Go Round

SWEETHEARTS this St. Valentine's Day, despite the May and December age difference, are Anne Leonard, 5, of 4584 Inverness, and Sun reporter Mac Reynolds. Mac "fell" for Anne, cute little starlet of the Sun-Ray Revue, when he covered the show recently. Here Anne reciprocates the affection on the appropriate day, with the appropriate gift — a Valentine box of candy.

STRICTLY PERSONAL

Valentine From Mac To Anne, 5

By MAC REYNOLDS

Strictly personal letter to Anne Leonard, age five:

DEAR ANNE:

After looking at our picture, I wonder what you see in me?

Photographer Dave Buchan took it. I think he's jealous.

Thank you for the Valentine and the heart-shaped box of chocolates. How did you know I liked toffee centres?

For that, I shall carve our initials in a live oak tree, or at least in the city editor's desk.

Let people point. Sure there's a little bit of difference in age, but after all, when you are 100 I'll only be 121.

I really meant it when I asked you to be my Valentine after covering the Sun-Ray Revue, in which you were first on the end of the chorus line. Director Dadye Rutherford said you held the line together. I wanted to say in my review that I feared your heart belonged to Dadye, but I put in Uncle Ben instead, because I have to live with Uncle Ben, and not Dadye Rutherford.

Thank you very much for inviting me to come to live in your house at 4584 Inverness for a year. It's a nice little house. Have you broached this subject to your father?

I wouldn't dream of telling anyone else, Anne, but your Valentine helped heal an old wound.

Frankly, I used to hate Valentine Day, and the schoolroom with its huge red-and-white box with the slot on top. I used to hate it because I never got as many Valentines as the others, and never as fancy, and hardly ever from the sirens for whom I pined.

You've made up for all that.

But what about you? While you were bouncing about the stage with your infectious gaiety, I was in the black pit of the theatre, just a bobbling yellow pencil and a pair of soulful black eyes. At least I think they were soulful.

Were you disappointed? Did you expect a Prince Charming and then find another Uncle Fred?

I thought you looked pretty cute anyway, in your blue snowsuit with the blue-and-white corsage and your light brown hair snuggled under the peekaboo bonnet and the dusting of freckles across your nose.

Your Valentine was cute, too. What could better describe our feelings than: "WHEW! Sure could LIKE you. Yes sir, Mister! 'N say, I DON'T mean . . . LIKE A SISTER."

Yes sir, Anne.

★ ★ ★

MAC REYNOLDS

HOSPITAL PLAN CHANGES FORECAST

$4.5 Million Surplus for B.C. Last Year, House Advised

By Sun Staff Reporter

VICTORIA, Feb. 14.—British Columbia's treasury collected a record $92,000,910 in the fiscal year ending last March 31 and after paying out $2,981,746 on Fraser Valley flood relief costs, over and above normal appropriations, finished the year with a surplus of $4,564,946.

This was shown today when Finance Minister Herbert Anscomb tabled public accounts at the opening of the Legislature.

Revenue collections soared by $25 million over the previous year, partly because of the newly-imposed 3 percent sales tax during the year and partly due to general buoyancy of all revenue sources. They exceeded the government's estimates by $15 million.

On the expenditure side, estimates were overspent by $10 million and were $24 million greater than in the previous year.

BUDGETS COMPARED

Here in brief is the comparative budget picture over the two years:

1947-48 — Revenue, $67,077,739; expenditure, $63,475,696.

1948-49 — Revenue, $92,000,910; expenditure, $87,435,963.

Biggest single source of revenue for the government was the yearly grant from Ottawa in lieu of the income tax. It amounted to $22,972,814.

Next in order was liquor profits, which produced $18,085,680 for the provincial coffers.

MOTORISTS SHELL OUT

Motorists shelled out a whopping $16,321,505, of which $10,191,179 was in gasoline taxes and $6,130,331 in license fees. Gas tax collections were up $900,000 from the previous year and license receipts up $500,000.

The sales tax, which operated only eigh months of the year, produced $14,335,110, which was entirely new revenue.

Other major sources of revenue included $7,458,000 from timber royalties and sales, an increase of $1 million; $1,948,688 from the amusement tax, which is a $1.5 million increase because the province took over the Dominion's wartime amusement levy of 25 percent; $1,005,754 from the fuel oil tax, an increase of $35,000, and $1,262,422 from land registry fees.

The accounts disclosed 1948-49 was B.C.'s biggest spending year in history to date. Total outlays for all purposes amounted to $119,679,000.

Please Turn to Page Two
See "Revenue"

$1000 FACT

Single Clue May Convict Murderer

It requires only a mite of correct information for trained police investigators to dispel the cloak of mystery which surrounds Vancouver's unsolved mysteries, to bring a slayer to justice.

You may have that vital information, but for fear of reprisal have failed to pass it on to police.

Under The Vancouver Sun's "Somebody Knows" plan you need have no fear.

Your identity remains concealed, your information may bring a slayer to justice and, if it does, you will be paid $1000.

The money will be paid in cash and you will remain anonymous.

Here is how you go about it:

Print or type your information on a plain sheet of paper. At the top of the sheet place any nine-digit code number. In a lower corner of the letter place the same number and tear it off.

Put this fragment of paper in a safe place. It may be worth $1000 to you.

Mail your letter to "Somebody Knows," Box 1200, The Vancouver Sun, 500 Beatty Street, Vancouver, B.C.

If yours is information that leads to the arrest and conviction of a murderer, your code number will be published in The Sun.

To collect your reward, bring the torn corner of your letter to The Sun, match up the code number and the fragment and you will be paid $1000 in cash.

No questions will be asked.

Particulars of another unsolved Vancouver slaying on Page 7.

Storm to Hit City Tonight

Vancouver experienced its warmest night in seven weeks last night.

The mercury stayed above 40, the first time since December 29. This area was the warmest in the province.

A storm gathering momentum 700 miles off the coast is expected hit Vancouver tonight, bringing heavy rain and wind.

Gale warnings have been issued for all exposed waters.

By LESLIE FOX
Sun Staff Reporter

VICTORIA, Feb. 14.—Changes in British Columbia's Hospital Insurance Act at the coming session of the Legislature to improve operation of the scheme were definitely promised by the government for the first time today.

The pledge came in the Speech from the Throne read by Lieut.-Governor Charles A. Banks at the opening of the session this afternoon.

The speech gave no hint of the exact nature of the changes proposed by the government, other than to say they would have the object of "improving administrative procedures."

However, it is thought they may include compulsory payroll deductions for hospital insurance premiums in place of the present voluntary system.

NEW COMMISSION

There is also speculation the government will propose a new form of commission be set up to run the service, possibly with two assistant commissioners to aid Lloyd F. Detwiller, recently-appointed commissioner.

Also disclosed in the Throne Speech is that the government is proposing a new control scheme for the Fraser Valley dyking system.

The dykes were all rebuilt after the devastating 1948 floods. The new scheme, details of which were not given, will be to handle the maintenance of the flood barriers. It may involve a different system of dyking districts.

The speech also announced that the government is planning "a closer liaison" with the native Indians of the province, who last year were given the voting franchise for the first time.

It is expected this will involve the appointment of an official who will look after matters concerning the Indians that are not handled by the federal Indian Affairs department.

HOUSING BILLS

Other legislation foreshadowed by the Throne Speech, which bears out previous forecasts, includes:

Two housing bills, one to authorize provincial cooperation with the Dominion in its low-cost housing scheme, and the other to enable cities and municipalities to participate. These have already been thoroughly talked over at conferences both here and in Ottawa.

Please Turn to Page Two
See "Legislation"

Crash-Landed Off Vancouver Island

Forty Canadian and American air-sea rescue craft fought today through gale winds and rain off the north tip of Vancouver Island in a massive search for a lost B-36 bomber and its crew of 17.

The giant plane, with one engine ablaze and another acting badly, splashed into the sea at about 3:30 a.m. today while winging southward along the B.C. coast from Alaska, bound for Texas.

The bomber is officially "missing." Its crew of 16 and one passenger, U.S. Air Force officials hope, have taken to liferafts.

Gales up to 40 miles an hour and rain envelop the search scene, Queen Charlotte Sound, a bare 200 to 300 miles north northwest of Vancouver.

DESTROYER ON WAY

Survivors, if any, would be clinging to life rafts, drenched by charging seas, and their chances of survival are uncertain.

But a huge two-nation search force was speeding to the scene.

Thirty-four planes, including seven Vancouver-based RCAF craft and 10 B-29 Superfortresses, are covering the area from the air.

The Canadian destroyer, HMCS Cayuga, heading northward at full steam from Esquimalt, is due to reach the search area by 8 p.m. tonight.

Three RCAF high speed launches were expected to be in the stormy Sound by 2 p.m. this afternoon.

HELICOPTER TO AID

And a Vancouver helicopter, operating from a towed scow in a unique search method, will shortly join the search force.

One RCAF craft, badly iced up, turned back to base after a morning takeoff. The helicopter landed at Comox for hasty mechanical repairs on its way north.

Port Hardy, on the northern tip of Vancouver Island, has been designated the main search base. There, planes and boats which are able to use the base will refuel.

Weather at Port Hardy was hampering the search, making it impossible to launch boats.

"The B-36 couldn't last a minute, if she broke open in these seas," said a B.C. Police officer at Port Hardy.

One report said two of the giant plane's six engines had lost power, and a third had been feathered just before it "ditched."

The crippled bomber, en route from Eilson Air Force Base, Alaska, to Fort Worth, Texas, sent three distress signals shortly after midnight as it winged southward off the B.C. coast.

DANGEROUS ICING

The first message reported the bomber was encountering dangerous icing at a 16,000 and 17,000 foot altitude.

Another message told of "instrument and engine trouble; severe emergency. Going to let down through overcast to lose ice."

Listening "ham" radio operators and other stations along the coast finally heard the plane signal:

"One engine on fire; contemplating ditch in Queen Charlotte Sound, between Queen Charlotte Island and Vancouver Island.

"Keep a careful lookout for flares or wreckage."

The plane was the second B-36 ever to have been lost, and the fourth plane to crash in British Columbia, or adjacent to this province, in the past 19 days.

BCE Plans $3.5 Million Hydro Work

A $3,500,000 plan to modernize Lake Buntzen hydro-electric plant number one was announced today by B.C. Electric president A. E. Grauer.

Work is scheduled to start in May and the project will be completed in the autumn of 1951. The new plant will have a capacity of 72,000 horsepower compared with 28,000 there today.

It will be used during peak periods in the winter season, BCE chief engineer and vice-president Thomas Ingledow said.

The company disclosed that a $500,000 contract for the 72,000 horsepower turbine has been let to Vancouver Engineering Works. A vertical reaction-type turbine, the new machine will be 35 feet in diameter and have a speed of 240 revolutions per minute. One of the giant valves will measure more than 11 feet in diameter.

This, together with an 84-inch valve and other auxiliary equipment, will all be built at Vancouver Engineering.

In awarding the work to a city firm, Mr. Grauer said, "This contract was let after a number of bids had been received. It is very pleasing to see that a Vancouver firm can successfully compete with price and quality with the long-established eastern companies.

"As the remainder of our 1950 construction program gets under way in the spring, this will further assist employment in B.C. and Canada to the extent of $22 million."

Mr. Ingledow said the new unti will replace seven existing generating units, two of which have been pumping energy into Vancouver since 1903.

Unconscious For 8 Days

Vina McHaffie, 19, of 2330 Carolina, is still fighting desperately for her life as she spends her eighth day in unconciousness.

She suffered serious head and internal injuries when she was involved in a traffic accident at Carolina and Broadway February 6.

Her condition in General Hospital today is "poor."

TOKYO, Japan, Feb. 14 —(BUP) — Margaret Sanger, the famed American birth control advocate, has been barred from entering Japan for a lecture tour, a spokesman for the Tokyo newspaper Yomiuri said today.

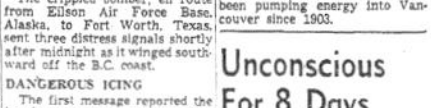

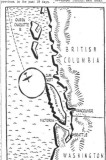

ROUTE of the U.S. Air Force B-36 bomber which is down somewhere between the Queen Charlottes and Vancouver Island is shown in map.

Front page of *The Vancouver Sun*, 14 February 1950. *Credit: Vancouver Sun*

twelve from the front section were out in ten seconds. The five in the rear compartment were out in from five to three seconds. It is known that every man left the aircraft. The pilot was able to see Mount Cardin before abandoning the aircraft. The last man out of the rear compartment landed at 53.05N by 129.07W.

RCAF Search & Rescue Report, Operation Brix, February 1950.

Captain Barry told reporters soon after the accident that he had set the "automatic pilot and somehow it turned in the air and came back over us." He also said he knew what the aircraft was doing in the dark as "there were three engines burning and I could follow the ship's progress as I went down in my chute."

S/Sgt. James Ford recalled the night on the island: "We made a teepee out of a parachute and I remember that we emptied our pockets and wallets of any paper we had to make a fire, except money. Once we got the fire going, we tried to dry our socks and get warm, but it was a pretty miserable night, although I didn't even come down with a cold after all that exposure."

Lt. Ray Whitfield also recalls surviving the bailout. In his 31 July 1998 interview done by Don Pyeatt, Whitfield tells that a tree snagged his parachute and that he hung in the darkness as he could not see the ground. Eventually his parachute ripped, and he dropped until another branch snagged him. He says his eyes adjusted to the darkness, and he could soon see the ground, at which point he released himself from the parachute harness and dropped down a steep slope. He took shelter under a rock overhang, wrapped himself in the parachute and slept for a short time.

In that interview, Whitfield further recalls that at daylight he moved downhill to look for a stream to follow to the coast so that he would be visible to any search and rescue effort. He met Captain Barry after hearing Barry fire a pistol. An hour later, after becoming colder and wetter, they found the radio operator Sgt. Trippodi. Following are comments from Lt. Ray Whitfield:

Trippodi [was] hanging upside down from the top of a cliff. He had impacted the cliff face and his chute had snagged the edge of the cliff. Dazed, he evidently released the top of his harness from the chute before releasing the bottom and flipped upside down.

His foot became snagged in the cord and he hung there in the cold wind until we found him. Barry reached him before I did and pulled him from the cliff. We found a dry recess in the rocks and made him a bed of tree branches. We made a fire and warmed him up, gave him our rations, and stayed with him. He was very weak and almost delirious. After a long miserable night we realized no one would find us while we were in that location and that Trippodi's only hope was for Barry and me to continue to the coast to find help. The decision for both of us going was based on our survival training that taught us to never strike out alone to find help. A single person will often not survive the journey. Barry and I continued to the coast. Once there we stamped out an SOS in the snow on the beach and filled the impressions with tree boughs so as to make them more visible from the air. We arrived at the coast completely soaked and very cold. Several hours passed and then we saw a local fishing boat and hailed to it. We were spotted and rescued and a mountain team was sent to find Trippodi. They found him near death from exposure but managed to remove him from the mountain.

Several United States' military aircraft had crashed in the Pacific Northwest in the first two months of 1950. The worst was a missing C-54 transporter with forty-four men aboard. Three aircraft would crash during the search for this one airplane. Aside from the B-36 and the B-29 that crashed during the search, the U.S. Air Force also lost two jet fighters in an aerial collision in Alaska.

Rescued

The Canadian and U.S. militaries conducted what was probably the largest ever search effort. Over forty aircraft were involved, and more were on stand-by. The Canadian military launched search and rescue Operation Brix, but were told nothing of the atomic bomb.

British Columbian newspapers reported on 14 February that more than thirty vessels and aircraft were working out of Port Hardy in the massive search. But the traditionally bad weather of the Charlottes was said to be hampering the search. By that morning, the RCAF 12 Group HQ at the Jericho RCAF Depot had already established an operations center for the mission, and Vancouver res-

Ten of the survivors at Port Hardy. *Credit: RCAF/DND*

General John Montgomery (left) and unknown officer. *Credit: U.S. Air Force*

ident Flight Lt. Gordon Bell-Irving was placed in charge of what would become Operation Brix.

What the newspapers did not report was that Brig. General John Beverly Montgomery, the director of operations for Strategic Air Command, had flown in to Vancouver to be on the spot if anything about the atomic mission was about to be compromised.

In conjunction with the RCN and RCAF, the USAF sent ten long-range patrol aircraft and several B-29 bombers; the U.S. Navy sent twelve Neptune long-range patrol aircraft; and the U.S. Coast Guard sent another six aircraft. Within minutes of the emergency broadcast, aircraft had been dispatched from RCAF Station Sea Island near Vancouver, and U.S. helicopters were sent to an area near Surf Inlet on Princess Royal Island.

In the beginning, the RCAF had very little information. They knew that at 23:30 local time aircraft #92075 was letting down to lose ice, and that five minutes later it was heading out to sea to lose ice. They also knew that at 23:40 it had one engine on fire and the crew was contemplating bailing out. Contact was lost after the crew reported losing one more engine at 23:41.

During the first day of Op Brix the southern tips of Estevan and Campania Islands were covered completely. It was during this initial search that the U.S. military found a small oil slick "one mile long [1.6 km] 50 to 70 feet [15–20 m] wide with position of center of slick 52°26' N, 129°3' W." This was soon determined to be unrelated and probably caused by a local fishing boat.

In the first days of the operation, the military took seriously the reports of the B-36 over Vancouver Island and extended the search to the entire island and the waters ninety kilometers (56 mi.) west. However, the search was almost immediately truncated when reports arrived of the rescue of the first two survivors. Op Brix reports that "some survivors were found before the search got well underway. At 1300 PST two survivors were found on Princess Royal Island. Nine more survivors were found during the remainder of the afternoon and another was found 16 February."

According to RCAF Op Brix official report, "Then, the next day, came the sudden break. A fishing vessel, the "Cape Perry," sighted smoke on the beach of Princess Royal Island. Closing the island, the skipper saw figures walking on the rocky shoreline. Minutes later came the flash: Survivors from the B-36 had been found."

The ten most mobile survivors gathered in three groups near the coast in hope of being spotted. Whitfield recalls seeing the local fishing boat and hailing it. "We were spotted and rescued and a mountain team was sent to find Trippodi. They found him near death from exposure but managed to remove him from the mountain." Trippodi was injured and not brought out with the ten.

"We later spotted boats but could not attract their attention. We started down coast to where we lit a signal fire to make plenty of smoke," said Captain Harold Barry.

Captain Barry told his story to the International News Service within hours of returning to the United States. He said:

> I'm not sure just what happened. We were flying along at about 15000 feet [4,500 m]. We began losing airspeed and altitude and I was pretty sure we were icing up. I asked our radar man to find the nearest land and I put the ship over what I hoped was it. I ordered the crew to bail out and away they went. I was the last man out. The ship was on autopilot and somehow it turned in the air and came back over us. There were three engines burning and I could follow the progress as I went down in my chute. But I don't know where she crashed. I landed in a little pond with a thin crust of ice on it. I got pretty wet and so did my chute. It didn't do me much good for warmth during the rest of the night. I tried to build a fire but couldn't. I was pretty hungry and when I saw a ground squirrel I fired at him twice with my .45 but missed both times. But my shots attracted Lt. Whitfield, my navigator. He blew his whistle and we worked towards one another. Wednesday morning Whitfield built a fire and threw a lot of wood on it. That was the smoke the fishing boat saw. I was so happy when I saw that boat coming I didn't know what to do. It had been so long since I had been warm or well-fed I had forgotten what it was like.

The first ten had been picked up by Vance King of Horseshoe Bay, captain of the Canadian Fishing Company's boat MV *Cape Perry*. King stated that "the men had been out in the pouring rain for 24 hours and were soaked through. They were wet, tired, and looked pretty grim, but none seemed seriously injured. All were very hungry."

In spotting the smoke, King said at first he thought it was a forest fire, but then realized that all the snow and rain on the island made that nearly impossible. That was when he brought the *Cape*

A MIGHTY B-36 BOMBER, greatest global-bombing weapon of the U.S., is feared down at sea off B.C. coast with 17 persons.

Storm Hides Fate Of B-36, 17 Men

Aquitania To End Days On Scrap-Pile

SOUTHAMPTON, Eng. — (CP) — The 44,866-ton liner Aquitania, once the queen of Britain's merchant fleet, has been sold for salvage.

The Cunard Steamship Company announced the four-funnel liner, built in 1913, will be delivered to the British Iron and Steel Corporation (Salvage) Limited.

The Aquitania, a troop ship during the war, ended her days running displaced persons between here and Halifax. On Dec. 17, 1948, she completed her 443rd transatlantic voyage, having travelled 3,000,000 miles and carried 1,200,000 passengers.

Flaming Bomber Down Off B.C. Coast

Gale-swept waters or treacherous mountains of the Queen Charlottes, 350 miles north of Vancouver, today hid the fate of a giant U.S. Air Force B-36 bomber with 17 men aboard.

News that the big plane was missing early today touched off one of the biggest air searches in years, with RCAF, Royal Canadian Navy, U.S. Coast Guard, U.S. Navy and Air Force units taking part.

This afternoon at least 50 surface craft and planes were working out of Port Hardy near the northern tip of Vancouver Island.

Traditional bad weather of the Queen Charlottes is hampering the search.

Planes are being up badly at 2350 feet, visibility nine-tenths, wind nil, surface smooth and overcast, with snow squalls up to 40 mph.

But an estimated 450 men with latest search equipment are doing what they can.

Advance search headquarters has been set up at Port Hardy, which has a landing field, harbor and radio communication.

Further Slides Feared

Warning that rising temperatures may bring new snow slides was given today at rail cross closed slides which held up traffic Monday.

CPR reported its line open this morning, and three passenger trains, trapped between Yale and Boston Bar at Saddle Rock, will reach Vancouver today. Eastbound traffic will also resume on schedule.

CNR expected late today to clear an slide-blocked line where ...steeping foreman John Turpac of Kamloops died in an avalanche Monday.

PGE, however, reported slides had halted traffic indefinitely.

Vancouver had its warmest night in six weeks overnight. Minimum temperature was 40.

Snoqualmie Pass, north of Seattle, was reported blocked with snow today. Ballderos and snow-plow equipment were working to clear the road.

HEAVY, WET SNOW

Temperatures in the Cariboo were actually in the high thirties or warmer at some places, with a high of 48 where it usually runs below zero freezing levels at 5000 feet.

Rock cliff near Cache Creek.

Bitter cold, storm warning ...

REAL CENTRE

But the mobile efficient "operations centre" at Jericho RCAF depot is the real centre. There Group Captain J. A. Easton, OBE, commanding officer of RCAF Maritime Group, in charge of the international search force. Vancouver's P.O., Lt. Gordon Sutliving at operations officer.

Under their direction, planes sweeping north, scanning mountains of sad Vancouver Island, dropping down at Port Hardy, then sweeping out over the ocean toward Queen Charlotte Sound.

Coastal mountains and the rugged slopes of the Queen Charlottes at search lines are being directed out.

FAST ORGANIZATION

The search was organized before it was definitely known the plane was missing.

U.S. Air Force officials here agreed today that the sea-engagements similar in the craft which crossed New sea ... contact Hawaii to Fort Worth and Rapid City, Texas.

First indications the plane was in trouble came early today when U.S. officials announced a B-36 had developed engine trouble over B.C. waters.

The craft was on its way from Alaska to Fort Worth, Texas.

THREE MESSAGES

Later it became known that three terse messages were sent from the B-26.

The first said the fire in three engines and had using condition at 14,000 to 17,000 feet.

The second gave a position north of Port Hardy, and out of engine trouble, faulty instruments and ice.

There was a silence, then the radio announced cryptic that the pilot was considering "ditching" the craft. That was the last word.

By Ivor Suttle, US Air Force and Navy planes were streaking for the area.

The last two radio messages were:

"At 17,666 feet, Severe head and instrument trouble; severe icing; two of three engines knocked out, three engines on fire ..."
(Continued on Next Page)

[map — BRITISH COLUMBIA / SEARCH AREA / VANCOUVER ISLAND / VICTORIA]

PRECEDENT SET

Indians Help 'Open' House

(Report of throne speech, news stories on House opening on Page 9.)

By GORDON ROOT
From The Vancouver Daily Province Victoria Bureau

VICTORIA—With all of the traditional pageantry and several colorful innovations, the first session of B.C.'s twenty-second Legislature was officially opened this afternoon.

In accordance with time-honored practice, members and guests on the floor of the House and the packed galleries heard Lt.-Gov. Banks read the throne speech. Attorney-General Wismer introduce the first legislation, and the presentation of reports by each of the 11 cabinet ministers.

In traditional fashion the House chose a new Speaker, but tradition was shattered when Mrs. Nancy Hodges (Coalition, Victoria) mounted the dais.

(Government Forecast)

TODAY

Intermittent rain becoming rain mixed with snow tonight. Continuing mild. Light winds increasing to E 20 this evening.
WEDNESDAY: Rain mixed with snow showers, Winds S 15 in the morning.

RECORDED TEMPERATURES
High Monday	 52
Low overnight	 40

FORECAST TEMPERATURES
High today	 46
Low tonight	 38
High Wednesday	 45

U.K. Election 'Who's Who' In Province

Who's who in the British election?
Peter Inglis of The Daily Province London Bureau tells the "inside" story of U.K. party leaders and top men of the election scene in a series of dispatches to be published between now and voting day, Feb. 23.
Today's sketch is of Labor Prime Minister Attlee. Read it on Page 2.

Parachuting Bridge Leaper Badly Hurt

PASADENA, Calif. — (INS) —Robert L. Stine of Oakland, and the youth who survived a 230-foot leap from the Golden Gate in a parachute, was reported in serious condition at County General Hospital today when he suffered critical injuries while attempting a similar parachute leap from Pasadena's drought... ...30,600,000 for payment of interest.

'HIDDEN WITNESS PLAN'

Whose Auto Killed Vancouver Janitor?

Whose auto killed J. E. Saunders?
The Daily Province HIDDEN WITNESS PLAN today offers a reward of much public concern as did the traffic death. For this reason, the HIDDEN WITNESS PLAN offers $1000 reward for information leading to conviction of the driver and guaranteed...

B.C.'s Liquor Bill Totals $57 Million

VICTORIA—B.C. spent almost $57,000,000 on liquor in the last year in the fiscal year ended March 31, 1949.

About $30,000,000 of the total went in provincial and Dominion governments as taxes and profits.

Here is the breakdown: Provincial liquor store profits, $18,450,000; Dominion taxes and duties, $11,031,430; provincial sales tax, $1,025,333.

The remaining $27,000,000 went to distillers and brewers and for handling charges.

Churchill Proposes Stalin Talk

EDINBURGH—(Reuters)—Winston Churchill hinted tonight that if he again becomes prime minister after the Feb. 23 general election, he will personally approach Prime Minister Stalin of Russia "in a supreme effort" to end the cold war.

Speaking to a huge election meeting, he recalling his earlier relations with Stalin and said:

"Still I cannot help coming back to this view of another talk with Soviet Russia upon the highest level.

IDEA 'APPEALS'

"The idea appeals to me of a supreme effort to bridge the gulf between the two worlds, so that without the horrid of the cold war."

He thousands surged outside Edinburgh's Usher Hall, unable to obtain admission, an overflow audience a mile away listened in by radio relay as Churchill ...

"It is my belief that this superiority in the atom bomb, if not indeed almost the monopoly of it that frightful weapon, in American hands is the surest guarantee of world peace tonight."

The Communist tonight has far the greatest military force, Churchill said, but the U.S. has the atom bomb—"and now we are told that they have a thousand-and-had more terrible manifestations of this awful power."

"It is my earnest hope that we may find our way to some such policy in world affairs.

(Continued on Next Page)
(See STALIN)

Revenues Surpass Expectation

From The Vancouver Daily Province Victoria Bureau

VICTORIA — B.C.'s revenues for 1949-49, estimated at $77,630,-665 in the budget for the year actually totalled $82,000,000.

Figures contained in public accounts for the fiscal year, filed today in the Legislature, show, however, that expenditure, estimated at $77,000,000, finally amounted to $87,400,000.

The revenue surplus for the 12-month period was $4,600,000, and the revenue surplus fund at March 31, 1949, totalled $8,000,000. During the year $9,259,000 of the revenue surplus fund was used to rebuild hospitals, public buildings and roads, and another $22,000,000 was shifted from capital to borrowings.

In the 12 months ended March 31, the gross public debt of $133,060,000, servicing of the provincial sinking funds, and the net debt, $126,000,000 was used for debt.

Scandinavians Study Defence Against Bomb

STOCKHOLM — (Reuters) — Scandinavian defence against the hydrogen bomb was discussed by the prime ministers of Norway, Denmark and Sweden at their meeting Monday in Stockholm, Sweden.

The meeting was one of the routine conference between the three countries in for a common foreign policy, particularly in the United Nations.

It was the major one. It was mainly policies. Sweden remains "neutral" and Norway and Denmark members of the Atlantic Pact.

Gales, Rain Lash Britain

LONDON — (Reuters)—Many parts of Britain were flooded Monday after an avalanche of gales and rain.

For the fifth day coastal shipping was held up in the Thames Estuary and through the Straits of Dover.

London has 2.4 inches of rain over total rainfall for February. One of the worst-hit towns was Worcester, at the west of England, where the River Severn was over than 12 feet above the normal. Police stationed in crisis overrode homes.

Snow fell in northern England and snow gusts in Scotland were covered with snow.

Province Writer Rides A "Rocket"

By ROSS MUNRO
Vancouver Daily Province War Writer

WHITEHORSE, Yukon—What's it like to fly in a jet fighter at more than 500 miles an hour?

What's it like to ride a rocket straight up from a few hundred feet off the ground to 10,000 feet in two minutes and roll over completely at 20,000 feet above the Yukon Mountains?

We found out Monday. We rode in a cockpit behind the pilot of an American F-80 "Shooting Star" on operations in Exercise "Sweetbriar" and whistled past the 500 mark which puts you in a zone that lies close enough to the mysterious sonic barrier —the speed of sound—to be interesting.

This is nothing for jet pilots, the new elite of defence forces. But it is a unique experience for this correspondent who looks like most people that 40 mph is plenty—in a car.

In the pilots' room of the allied base here, crowded with Canadian and American jet pilots, we slipped into a parachute and donned the plastic headgear of the American fighter men which looks like a football helmet.

We bundled out to the sleek F-80, parked on the tarmac in 30 below zero conditions. The year-old Major Vance Poppleton, commander of the Scottsbank Fighter Squadron in Alaska which is equipped the Canadian-American zone here.

DRAINAGE PLANE

Three planes normally are single-seaters but this one had another cockpit rigged in it for training jet men. American airmen snapped us to the seat, which is one of emergency shoots you clear out of the plane.

The major started his engines with a hot-hum of a bot-fire, there was a gramble and a whine. We moved slowly, such a gentle swaying motion through the snow to the runway.

Named Two Zero except for takeoff, the major told us the control tower.

With an effortless pickup and long into the F-80 zipped down the runway, In a few seconds we were doing 150 mph. There was little vibration, no shaking. At first, we felt 300 in less than a minute.

500 FEET PER MIN.

"At 50" our rate of climb is 5000 feet a minute," said the major up front, who kept up a running commentary on events of the plane to pneumatic and as convincing as if he was demonstrating an automobile.

This plane is instrument of the F-80 which the RCAF will get later this year to replace their present Vampires.

The engine now available like a huge kettle on the boil, the shot through smiling sound of a snaky whine. I looked out to the front row. The snow-coated mountains whipped by in a dazzling sight...
(Continued on Next Page)
(See MUNRO)

Editor Held In Quebec 'Red' Raids

MONTREAL — (CP) — Pierre Gelinas, 25, editor of the French-language Labor newspaper, Le Combat, was among eight persons arrested Monday in anti-subversive squad detectives in two separate raids.

Seven men and a woman were arrested.

A high police official wanted Montrealers to beware of the Communist organization "Association Des Combattants De La Liberte" (Freedom Fighters' Association). He said it is "positively Communist-controlled."

CHARLIE BOUND

Paul Crepeau, organizer of the association, said:

"I am deeply shocked. The report that our organization a Communist is not true. I am not a Communist. I am a Roman Catholic.

Dr. We know there are some Communists in the organization but not know how we should stop them. We do not make any dictatorship, but if there should be any political party who refer passing party ..."

Gelinas and a woman identified as Mrs. Alphonse Mineault, 41, were charged as petitioning publications from door to door with out a permit.

Police said they found a pamphlet, and thanks for joining the association on their person.

SIX MORE ARRESTS

Six other men arrested were identified as Alfred Belanger, 25, Fred Devreau, 49; George Lajzerowicz, 43; Lucien LeBlanc, 25; Alfred Derhanie, 27, and James O'Neil, 45.

Police said they were arrested as they had a meeting at the headquarters of Harry Binder, declared LPP candidate in Montreal-Cartier riding of this last federal election.

Mr. Binder, said the building was being used as headquarters for the Montreal Council of Unemployed.

Mr. Binder was not present at the time of the raids.

Chinese, Russians Sign Pact

TOKYO — (AP) — The Peiping radio said today Communist Red China and Russia, have signed a 30-year treaty of friendship and alliance.

A broadcast heard in Tokyo said purpose of the treaty was "to prevent a rise in Japanese imperialism" and "any new aggression that might be launched by any country directly or indirectly in concert with Japan."

Atom Board Chief Named

WASHINGTON — (INS) — President Truman today selected Sumner T. Pike as acting chairman of the Atomic Energy Commission.

Pike, a member of the commission, and the only remaining original member of the group, will succeed David E. Lilienthal, who retires Wednesday.

Traffic Tips

These tips on winter driving are passed on by the Queen Charlotte motorists.

Start slowly and easily.
Keep a careful lookout for flares or wreckage.

HEAVY SEAS

Air bases and Coast Guard establishments up and down the coast from Alaska to San Francisco were alerted.

The weather, ranging from heavy rain from Alaska north, and another message from Port Hardy. All roads into...

CRASH BOATS

The RCAF and up to seven planes supported by crash rescue vessels.

Two high-speed crash boats left Patricia Bay.

The three ship, RCAF supply vessel Stanghar, will steamline a new technique in rescue operations. She is towing a new "Sea King" flying boat on most of its mercy of the north.

B.C. Appeals On Doukhobor Sentences

Special to The Daily Province
VICTORIA—The B.C. Government today asks the appeal court to restore "severe" prison terms imposed on seven Sons of Freedom Doukhobors.

The men were convicted of arson and threatening of destroying property over the last year, were given light sentences by County Judge Manson Friday at Nelson.

They ranged from 24 hours to three months.

Attorney - General Wismer announced the department's intention to appeal.

The seven members of the Canadian-American sect were charged with the burning of a Blaine home and a school at Krestova, and were held on $5,000 fines.

Neck-and-Neck Race In Britain

By PETER INGLIS
From The Vancouver Daily Province London Bureau

LONDON — Britain's Labor party and Conservatives are running neck-and-neck in the battle for votes the general election Feb. 23, which seems like one in which the balance in the House may again be held by the Liberals.

The current all-out claims by both sides that they will win are not borne out closer study of the facts.

The Liberals chiefly are hoping for a dead heat. Although the Conservatives give them little chance of gaining more than 50 seats, the Liberals do well in by-elections.

LIBERALS HOPE FOR DEAD HEAT

Labor manager Herbert Morrison and the bargaining would be for some measure of proportional representation.

Labor has slightly a lead in the popular vote but the Liberals hold the balance...

Three survivors of flight 075 awaiting repatriation to the U.S.A.
Credit: Department of National Defence

Perry as close to shore as possible for a better view. King saw a man near the fire waving vigorously and sent the dory ashore to pick up the first two men at about 12:30 lunchtime. About one kilometer (0.6 mi.) away they found a sole survivor, and then later spotted a fire and picked up another seven crewmen at about 1:15 p.m. "There, we discovered seven more men huddled around a fire. We had a bottle of rum and a bottle of scotch aboard and we gave them some drinks."

King and his crew transferred the ten men to a U.S. Coast Guard boat which arrived at 4:30 p.m. that afternoon. From there the men were transferred to a Canso for the flight to Port Hardy. The U.S. Coast Guard immediately informed the men that they were to refrain from speaking about the bomber and its mechanical problems. Their only statements would be confined to their survival and rescue.

In a bit of unknowing irony, the *Vancouver Sun* reported on the front page of their 15 February edition that "H-Bomb could wipe out World in Minute." Fortunately for the U.S. Air Force, no one had connected the flight with a nuclear mission.

In another section of the paper, Princess Royal Island was described by a zealous headline writer at the *Sun* as being "Wild

Animal-Infested." Given the rain and snow, the island was more accurately described as one big sponge.

One of the problems encountered by the search was that information about the final moments of the flight gathered from the crew often hampered the search. The RCAF found that data on the course (direction), position, altitude and order of bailout came to them from various offices and was "in some cases conflicting." One big problem was that initial data had 92075 flying at 165 degrees Magnetic, and searches were planned on this basis. With the assistance of a B-36 pilot on loan to the RCAF for Op Brix, they learned this was supposed to be 165 degrees True, and had to establish a new search plan.

In the United States, S/Sgt. Dick Thrasher had also told his story:

> First thing I knew the pilot said we couldn't hold our altitude any longer. He said we were over Princess Royal Island and to go ahead and bail out. Two men jumped ahead of me and I jumped. I landed in a big tree in the dark and I could not get loose from my parachute. I cut myself free with a knife. I spent the rest of the night in a one-man life raft. I was all by myself. The raft kept me dry. The next morning I was cold, so I climbed the tree to try to get my chute. When I got to the top of the tree I began yelling for all I was worth. The navigator and radio operator answered. We found another gunner, then we found another officer. We were so weak we decided to build a tent out of our parachutes and my life raft. After a lot of trouble we finally got a little fire going. We were lucky. We had our lighters and some lighter fluid but everything on the ground was wet and we had a hard time keeping the fire going through the second night. When morning came we decided to try to walk, and we found Captain Harold Barry and another man. We tramped an SOS in the snow and just started to build a fire when we heard a motor. Captain Barry and I walked down to the shore and began shooting flares. It was a Canadian fishing boat. I think this was about 2:30 p.m. Wednesday.

Cpl. Schuler said he "smacked into one [a tree], was knocked out, and on coming to made for the coast where [he] was finally picked up." Schuler was found alone on the beach. After him, a group of seven men were found by the *Cape Perry*. Lt. Roy R. Darrah described the time on the island as "the most horrible night of my life."

The ten men were in Port Hardy at the RCAF airfield for less than two hours before boarding a USAF transport for their flight back to the States.

In 1997, prior to the gathering of the remaining survivors for a reunion, Vitale Trippodi of Brooklyn, New York, recalled the harrowing experience. He told of being found by Barry and Whitfield and being released from the tree. "But I couldn't walk because of frostbitten feet so they made me comfortable at the foot of the tree and told me that they couldn't stay with me; they had to go find help for the others, but that they would come back for me. I lay there in that ice and snow for a day or two until I was found by a Canadian rescue team, who got me to a ship." In fact, Trippodi was rescued the evening of 15 February, according to original declassified accounts of the rescue.

Lt. William Kidd of Vancouver and CPO E. Wooley of Langley Prairie, B.C., led the *Cayuga*'s sixteen-man rescue crew to retrieve Sergeant Trippodi. Surgeon LCdr. Andrew Weir and PO Alex Matte, a medical assistant, gave Trippodi a sedative, placed him on a Neil-Robertson stretcher and made him as comfortable as possible. In complete darkness they carried him off the mountain.

Sgt. Vitale Trippodi, the twenty-three-year-old from New York, also told his tale to the throng of reporters gathered to see the rescued men.

I was hanging there in that tree with a foot caught in a chute strap. I tried to get loose. After a few hours I didn't care anymore. I felt like I was dying. I would hang, head down, as long as I could, then I would reach out and grab a branch and pull myself sideways. But my arms would get tired and I'd let go. I tried to knock myself out, but I couldn't do it. All the time I hung there my Mae West [life preserver] was chocking me. I could not sleep any, I was just sort of dazed. When my pilot and my co-pilot pulled me down Tuesday and left me lying there I felt like I was dead. Those Canadians who picked me up were the swellest people I have ever met. The first thing they did was to give me morphine to kill the pain in my foot. Then I drank all their cocoa. Those Canadians are wonderful. I wouldn't be here if that rescue party hadn't spotted me.

The first ten survivors were picked up either by an RCAF Canso or by a U.S. Coast Guard PBY amphibious aircraft for the flight to Port

STRAINED FACES OF AIRMEN showed through the tired smiles of some of them as the 10 rescued fliers gulped steaming cups of coffee and waited for medical examinations at Port Hardy Wednesday after their terrible 34-hour ordeal. Seated (from left) are S/Sgt. James Ford, Haldenville, Okla.; Cpl. Richard Schuler, Miami; Lieut. Paul Gerhart, Lancaster, Penn.; Daniel Macdonald, Los Angeles; Sgt. Martin Stephens, Houston, Tex.; (standing, from left) Lieut. Ernest Cox, Pampa, Tex.; Lieut. Ray Whitfield, San Antonio, Tex.; Capt. Harold Barry, Hillsboro, Ill.; S/Sgt. Dick Thrashek, Chilton, Tex.; Lieut. Roy Darrah, Martins Ferry, Ohio.

—Pictures by Chuck Jones, Daily Province Staff Photographer

Twelve Airmen Saved From B-36

Captain's Story Of Crash

By CAPT. HAROLD L. BARRY
As Told to International News

McCHORD AIR FORCE BASE, Wash.—I'm not sure just what happened. We were flying at about 5000 feet.

We began losing air speed and altitude and I was pretty sure we were icing up. I asked our radar man to find the nearest land and I put the ship over what I hoped was it.

I ordered the crew to bail out and away they went. I was last out.

ENGINE BURNING

The ship was on the automatic pilot and somehow it turned in the air and came back over us.

There were three engines burning and I could follow the ship's progress as I went down in my 'chute.

But I don't know where she crashed.

I landed in a little pond with a thin crust of ice on it. I got wet pretty well and did my 'chute. It didn't do me much good for some warmth during the rest of the night.

I wrapped up in it and waited until daylight.

MISSED SQUIRREL

I tried to build a fire but couldn't. I was pretty hungry and when I saw a ground squirrel I fired at him twice with my .45 and missed both times.

But my shots attracted Lt. Whitfield, my navigator. He blew his whistle and we worked toward one another.

Whitfield and I struck for the beach. During Tuesday, we found seven other men.

That afternoon Whitfield and I spent two hours freeing Sgt. Vitale Trippodi, the ship's radioman, from a tree where he had hung, head down, for almost 12 hours.

IN BAD SHAPE

Trippodi was in pretty bad shape. When we got him out of the tree, we hurt didn't have the strength to move him down to the beach.

We spent all that night trying to keep warm and looking for something to eat.

Wednesday morning, Whitfield built a fire and we threw a lot of wood on it. Then we lay down in the flaming heap.

I was so happy when I saw that boat coming I didn't know what to do. It had been so long since I had been warm or well-fed I had forgotten what it was like.

Rescue Of Last Five Believed Near

(More pictures, stories on pages 3, 15, 26)

Twelve American fliers who bailed out of a burning B-36 bomber over desolate Princess Royal Island two days ago are safe.

Search parties were almost certain the remaining five men were alive and would be located today.

Distant cries for help and shots from inland on the isolated island intensified efforts of ground rescue crews to find the missing man.

The miraculous escape of the Americans was climaxed Wednesday when the Vancouver fish packer Cape Perry picked 10 hungry, haggard men from the beaches of Princess Royal Island, 400 miles northwest of Vancouver.

Later in day HMCS Cayuga, Canadian tribal destroyer, rescued the eleventh man, Staff-Sgt. Vitale Trippodi of Brooklyn, N.Y., only seriously injured man of the bomber crew. He was flown to Seattle at noon today by a U.S. plane.

When ground parties set out at dawn today to battle across back-breaking, rough terrain of the island, they were looking for six men.

A few hours later the report was flashed that a twelfth man had been found by Cayuga searchers. Suffering from a broken ankle he was taken on board the destroyer for treatment.

Name of the twelfth man was not known immediately.

In the greatest air, sea and land search in B.C.'s history, planes, ships and men of two nations are scouring the area for traces of the final five Americans.

"Find them all—but quick" was the order.

RCAF officials said at noon the situation "looks hopeful now for the other men."

The search, apparently wholly successful, was a costly one for eight other American fliers, who died when their B-36 search plane crashed in flames on take-off Wednesday from Spokane. Seven men survived.

LEGS MAULED

Treating the two injured survivors of the B-36 on board the Cayuga is Surgeon Lt.-Com. Andrew West of Esquimalt.

Most serious is Sgt. Trippodi, whose both legs are mangled and feared to be gangrenous.

Searchers include three parties from the Cayuga, one each from the American Coast Guard vessels Wynoma, Cahoone and Citron. RCAF para-rescue men, 20 Canadian army men from Victoria under Lieut. Mike Kearney, and five members of the Vancouver Alpine Club.

Weather in the search area was bad. Wind-driven snow cut visibility on the ground and in the air.

A U.S. Coast Guard plane, ranging over the island, was forced to put back to Port Hardy.

Snow added to the misery of the remaining survivors and searchers feared a heavy fall would cover injured men and make sighting of their white parachutes almost impossible.

SHIPS STAND BY

Rescue teams left their ships in the waters on the northern part of the island for the six men. Earlier reports that the men had been located have been denied.

The Americans strung out as they bailed out early Tuesday said the missing men were the first to leap from the six-engine bomber.

All through the night the Cayuga and the Wynoma stood by off the island kept searchlights playing and shot off flares to attract the attention of the survivors. Nor for that matter, was there any indication in it of higher taxes. Furthermore, there were no surprises.

(Continued on Next Page)
(See SEARCH)

SGT. TRIPPODI
... legs broken.

Eight Die In Chemical Explosion

(GOVERNMENT FORECAST)

MIDLAND, Mich. — Eight workers were killed and three others were reported missing in a terrific explosion which ripped the roof from a building of the Dow Chemical Company plant in Midland, Mich., today.

The blast shook the entire city of 10,000 and shattered windows over a large area. Roof of the building was blown sky high.

TRAPPED IN PLANT

The RCAF high speed launches, the Sturm and Montagnais, are moving from the Cayuga to take rescue groups ashore and bring the American survivors to the ship when found.

Commander of the Cayuga, which is directing operations, is Capt. M. A. Medland of Toronto. There are 185 men and officers on board.

Jobless Insurance To Broaden

By JOHN BIRD
From The Vancouver Daily Province Ottawa Bureau

OTTAWA — In contrast with the Speech From the Throne just one year ago, today's enclosed not the slightest hint of tax reduction.

Speaking through the Governor-General, the Liberal Government announced it will ask Parliament to widen the scope and extend the benefits of unemployment insurance.

It gave notice of amendments to the Agricultural Products Act, an Agricultural Prices Support

(Continued on Next Page)
(See HOUSE)

Parachuting U.S. Airmen Periled By Icy Ponds, Trees, Sheer Cliffs

By CHUCK JONES
Vancouver Daily Province Staff Photographer

PORT HARDY.—'It was the most horrible night in by life.'

First Lieutenant Ray P. Darrah spoke for his shivering, unshaven buddies as 15 silent U.S. airmen stood under the grey skies of Port Hardy airdrome, glad to be back, glad to be alive.

The time was 6:10 p.m. Wednesday.

Behind them were 34 terrible hours of anxiety, pain, fear and discomfort.

Ahead of them were steaming cups of coffee and medical examinations.

But the 19 just stood there, answering questions with a million unworded words or a shake of the head as they pulled rough, grey blankets around them in the chill darkness.

They didn't feel like talking. Just the odd word, as they stood there oblivious to the light-hearted talk of scores of excited U.S. and Canadian airmen who turned the gigantic search team which went into action minutes after their B-36 was reported missing Tuesday morning.

That was my first sight of the 10 survivors.

Less than two hours later I watched them clamber aboard a "Flying Boxcar" and disappear back into grey clouds on their way to Seattle and then their homes across America.

The time was 7:45 p.m.

I'm glad they got away fast from the memories of their 34 hours.

For flying up to Port Hardy from Vancouver Wednesday afternoon I got a slight taste of what they must have been up against.

With Vancouver's U-Op Pilot Ed Bell, I reached Port Hardy after flying through weather that varied from sudden, blinding sunshine to dense, dark clouds choked with rain, ice and snow.

Shortly after, the U.S. Coast Guard plane brought the 10 numbed survivors in from the Cape Perry, which had picked them up.

They told a story of bailing out in the inky, unknown skies over Princess Royal Island, of landing helter-skelter in trees, on cliffs and in ravines, of floundering out to the beaches through the forbidding terrain.

Drenching rains and thick snow, huge trees and boulders combined to make an almost unbeatable barrier in their march to the coast.

Some were injured, one seriously, most of them bruised and their haggard faces showed the strain of their ordeal.

Captain Harold L. Barry, Hillsboro, Ill., pilot of the big B-36, explained how all 15 crew members bailed out of the bomber after its engines caught fire.

"When we got near land we were rapidly losing altitude, so I put the plane in a slow turn, put it on the automatic pilot and got in line to bale out.

"Only myself and Co-pilot First Lieutenant Ray P. Whitfield, San Antonio, Texas, knew we were really in trouble.

"When I realized we would have to bale out I rang the alarm bell to notify the men to get ready to abandon ship.

"We had about seven minutes and I had the radar operator pick up a 'fix' on the coastal land. We got a three-mile fix from him.

"Lieutenant Whitfield made a tour of the plane to be sure everyone was okay. We found one man with his Mae West (life jacket) strapped on over the top of his parachute. He soon fixed that.

"About seven minutes later the boys started to hit the silk from the front and rear compartments.

"I was last out of the front compartment and First Lieutenant Darrah was last out of the rear compartment.

Lieutenant Darrah landed in a tree top only 15 yards inland from the icy seas of Queen Charlotte Sound.

"It was raining and snowing and blowing a gale all night long," said the officer. "I spent the night in the tree 16 feet up.

"Towards morning I started to shout and got an answer.

"It was First Lieutenant Ernest G. Cox, Pampa, Tex. Cox had also landed in a tree. 30 feet up, but had managed to get out of his 'chute and down to the ground.

"He made a bed and waited for daylight before starting out to find the owner of the voice.

"We could hardly see, but could not attract their attention in the dark, knew we were only 18 feet up.

"We later spotted boats but could not attract their attention. When we waited down we made a signal fire where we were and lit a signal fire to attract plenty of smoke.

"It was a rough trip. We walked about five miles and our flying clothes were so heavy with water we couldn't climb over logs. We just slit over or went around.

"We later discovered our

sopping clothes weighed 50 pounds apiece.

"We saw no sign of life on the tough train except a bear. I had only a knife between us and while we heard poor steaks were good eating, we weren't taking any chances tackling it.

"We were the first two spotted Wednesday, and as soon as we were aboard, the packer headed down the coast and picked up Cpl. Richard Schule, Miama, Fla., and finally a group of seven together."

Corporal Schuler was another victim of high trees.

"I smacked into one, was knocked out and on coming to made for the coast where I was finally picked up," said Corporal Schuler.

Tax Increase Suggested To Pay Hospital Costs

From The Vancouver Daily Province Victoria Bureau

VICTORIA—An increase of 2 percent in the sales tax to pay hospital insurance costs instead of collecting premiums was suggested in the Legislature Wednesday as a solution to the insurance scheme's financial headache.

"It is a debatable point," said Alex Hope (Coalition, Delta), who proposed the change.

"Old age pensioners and social service recipients are exempted from paying premiums, but there are many receiving war veterans' allowances and dependents who should be given consideration."

Both Mr. Hope and A. D. Turnbull (Coalition, Roseland-Trail) who referred to hospital insurance at the opening of the three-day debate on the throne speech debate, believed the public is satisfied with principles of the scheme.

Both attributed present difficulties to the fact that the scheme is new, and believed they would be ironed out as the staff gains experience.

On the Inside

"DADDY'S SAFE," cried happy wife of Lieut. Raymond P. Whitfield jr. in Fort Worth, Tex., when they heard he survived B-36 crash.

SURVIVAL STORY is told by First Lieut. Roy P. Whitfield, observer who ditched B-36 after he advised family he was safe.

LAST JUMP from burning B-36 was made by Pilot Capt. Harold L. Barry after he had told the crew to bail out.

ONE FOOT separated S/Sgt. James R. Ford from ground when his parachute caught in a tree as he landed after "ditching."

Lt. Raymond P. Whitfield Jr. getting out of the post-rescue transport aircraft.
Credit: U.S. Air Force

Crewman getting out of the post-rescue transport flight.
Credit: U.S. Air Force

Hardy on the northern tip of Vancouver Island. The records for the *Cayuga* claim it was a U.S. PBY aircraft, and the U.S. records claim it was an RCAF Canso. Regardless, in Port Hardy they were transferred to a U.S. Air Force C-82 'Flying Boxcar' for the flight to Tacoma, Washington, just south of the border. The flight back to Carswell AFB was not comforting as the twin-engined transporter lost one of its engines. Lt. Gerhart recalls seriously thinking "to hell with it!"

The search areas had to be limited. F/L Bell-Irving and his team reasoned that "from calculations based on the course and TAS of B-36 2075, and on the wind in the area at the time of the jump it was calculated that with a time lapse of 10 seconds between the first and last man (this lapse was the estimate of the survivors of the B-36), with the first man pulling his rip cord immediately and the last man pulling his rip cord 10 seconds after jumping, the first and last man would land 1.4 miles [2.2 km] apart. The last man would land SSE from the first man, that being the track of the aircraft during the jump. This indicated that survivors could not have landed on Gil Island or far inland on Princess Royal Island, yet the separation was sufficient for them to have landed in the water."

The conclusion was that since the survivors had landed in an area surrounding 53°02' N, 129°10'30" W, and since it was mainly those who jumped first who were missing, the missing must have landed in the water between Ashdown Island and Princess Royal Island.

The news on Wednesday, 15 February looked good, but had a dark side. The papers reported that nine men had already been found and that more had been seen by rescuers. However, a U.S. Air Force B-29 bomber taking off to join the search crashed in Montana, killing eight of the fifteen men on board.

Flight engineer Lt. C.G. Pooler was the last man rescued. He was seriously injured, having broken his ankle when he fell thirteen meters out of a tree. Still, he limped more than a kilometer (0.6 mi.) to a frozen lake and awaited rescue. He saw HMCS *Cayuga*'s searchlights, and knew he would soon be found.

In an interview between Pooler and Frank Perkins in the *Fort Worth Star-Telegram* 16 February 1997, the engineer recalled, "I had one of those search and rescue signaling mirrors and I got it out and began signaling a rescue plane that flew right over me. It flew right over me twice and I could see the reflections from my mirror dancing on its fuselage, but the crew never saw me and the plane flew on off. I remember digging out that candy bar and counting the squares and figuring out that if I ate one square of chocolate a day, I could eat for nine days."

On Thursday, 16 February he finally heard the voices of the ground search crew from the HMCS *Cayuga*. He had survived the broken bone and severe abrasions from the fall, but now was suffering from exposure. He was found at the edge of an uncharted lake by a rescue team led by Lt. De Rosenroll. However, it was no easy task to get him back to the ship. The three-kilometer (1.8-mi.) trip to the edge of the island, carrying the stretcher through the snow, took seven hours.

According to an article in the March 1950 issue of the *Crowsnest*, "Three teams were landed from *Cayuga*. Others were landed from the Coast Guard cutters, and Army and Air Force searchers added to the score. That afternoon the *Cayuga*'s first res-

Sgt. Trippodi being transported by motor boat from HMCS *Cayuga* to a waiting aircraft. Trippodi is seen in a Neil-Robertson stretcher accompanied by medical assistant PO Alex Matte (wearing glasses) and Surgeon LCdr. A. Weir who were part of the original rescue team.

Credit: Department of National Defence

cue team, led by Lt. G.M. De Rosenroll, of Calgary, heard faint cries in the distance. Slowly they made their way to the sounds. There, beside a small frozen lake, they found 1st Lt. Charles Pooler, USAF, lying with a broken ankle. Getting Lt. Pooler, the bomber's second engineer, back to the beach was a battle in itself. The rescue team had a mile and three-quarters [2.8 km] to go. It took them seven hours."

The RCAF final report in Op Brix stated "observer reports indicated that a large aircraft flew low over the west coast of Vancouver Island as far south as the Straits of Juan de Fuca immediately after the last report from 2075. The observer reports were later confirmed to be of B-36 92083, although this aircraft had flown at 17,000 feet [5,200 m]." The RCAF recommendation after the search and rescue operation noted, "twenty-five observer reports were received which gave an authentic plot of the track of B-36 2083. The estimated heights of these reports were completely inaccurate." The air force realized that people could not accurately determine how high a B-36 was flying, given the noise and vibration it would generate, even at a high altitude. This evidence helps to demolish the theory that people saw 92075 flying low over Vancouver Island and that others saw it flying low in northern B.C.

At least 5,810 man-hours were spent in the bush searching for the last seven crewmen during the nine days of the ground search. Although two more were found, five were forever lost.

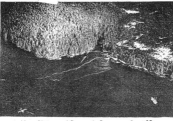

Ship or unit	Complement	Man-hours in bush
Cayuga	210	3,000
US Coast Guard cutters (6)	170	1,620
RCAF para-rescue squad	4	160
Canadian Army	28	890
Alpine Club of Vancouver	5	140

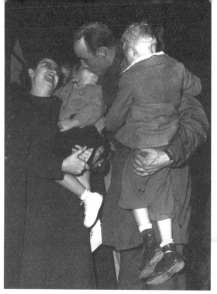

Cox kisses his daughter Vickie.
Credit: Forth Worth Star-Telegram

Richard Schuler greeted by press photographer Peggy Spencer, as he had no family to greet him on his return to Fort Worth, Texas.
Credit: Forth Worth Star-Telegram

Happy family reunion. *Credit: Forth Worth* Star-Telegram

James Ford with his parents and younger brother.
Credit: Forth Worth Star-Telegram

Stephens and his wife.
Credit: Forth Worth Star-Telegram

Weary B-36 Search Parties Find Comfort Aboard U.S. Coast Guard Vessel White Holly

MOST RUGGED COUNTRY they'd ever seen was the comment of these tired searchers who covered almost 15 miles on Princess Royal Island. Seen aboard USCG White Holly are, from left: Harold Geck, Paul Palker and Donald Idom, all of Ketchikan, Alaska; Roger Krona, Tacoma; Frank Akers, Curlew, Wash., and Bill Tipewold, Bethany, Ill.

POSSIBILITY one of five missing U.S. airmen used this liferaft after parachuting from B-36 bomber eight days ago has been raised. Fishermen George Reader of the fishing vessel Cape Bathurst holds the raft, fished by the boat from the waters of Whale Channel.

ALPINISTS' APPETITES were sharpened by rigorous search over Princess Royal Island's tough terrain, as these three members of Vancouver Alpine Club indicate after they asked USCG White Holly's cook Ken Gross what was in store. Charles Jenkins, Herman Genschorek and Fred Parkes give chicken cooking its path full approval. Vancouver men are assisting U.S. personnel in hunt for fliers.

ASK EDITH ADAMS
Sun Cottage, Homemakers' Service, 510 Beatty St. TA. 4577, MA. 1161. Listen to the "Edith Adams' Cottage of the Air" program, 3:30 to 3:45 a.m. every Tuesday and Thursday, CKNO.

Vancouver Pianist At Carnegie Hall

Gordon Manley Heard With Enthusiasm in New York

By PAT USSHER

NEW YORK, Feb. 21 — Gordon Manley, Vancouver pianist, gave his first Carnegie Hall concert Monday night before an enthusiastic audience.

The 26-year-old Canadian included works from Chopin, Beethoven, Debussy and Liszt on his program. He showed mastery of technique and artistry of expression.

VARIED PROGRAM

The program opened with Chaconne, by Bach-Busoni, Beethoven's Sonata in E Minor, Op. 90, followed and then three works by Chopin-Scherzo in C Sharp Minor, Op. 39; Impromptu in F Sharp, Op. 36, and Scherzo in B Flat Minor, Op. 31.

After the intermission Manley played four short Debussy pieces, including La Cathedrale Engloutie, and Liszt's Polonaise No. 2 in E.

The tall, dark-haired young pianist was called back three times for encores. Among the audience was a number of students from Aorta Old Farms School for Boys in Avon Conn., where he is director of the music department.

Manley, who made his professional debut at 15 in Vancouver, has played in New York before but his previous appearances were at Town Hall.

He studied at the Conservatory of Music in Toronto and in New York, has toured Canada, and recently made a four-month tour of Europe.

PARENTS HERE

Mr. and Mrs. John Manley, the pianist's parents, still live in Vancouver. Both are amazing musicians, his father on the violin and his mother the piano.

"I'm only sorry that they are not here tonight," he said in a brief interview after the concert.

"My favorite composers are those who write best for piano—Chopin, Debussy and Liszt. Of course, Chopin is a tough limit. He really uses the piano. He's so versatile."

GORDON MANLEY
. . . New York acclaims

Youth Groups Seek Abandoned School

A delegation of two from Kingcrest Chamber of Commerce Monday night asked Vancouver school board for permission to use abandoned school buildings at Twentieth and Clark for community youth purposes.

The Board told the delegation they would consider the request, though they have been considering other plans for the buildings.

The buildings in question were used during the war for recreation of training, but are now abandoned.

"There are an awful lot of kids up in our district who have no place to play," said delegation leader Gil Munro, of 1362 Kingsway.

He was backed by Johnny Cavalier, coach of the Burrard Lacrosse team.

"The Burrards need a room in which they can put a permanent punching bag and facilities for the boys," said Munro. "They have [fogged] a boxing ring from this school, but don't have a 'hand' has been given in this column.

Red Cross Fund Asks $500,000

March 1 Opening Date Set for 1950 Campaign

Arrangements have been completed for an intensive campaign to raise $500,000 as British Columbia's share of the $5,000,000 objective, set for 1950 for the Canadian Red Cross Society.

The campaign opens March 1. "The success of the annual Red Cross campaign is vital to carry on the work of Red Cross from year to year," said Hon. E. W. Hamber, provincial campaign chairman.

"While the main objective of Monday by the civic licences and claims committee following a complaint by the Retail Merchants' Association of "unfair business practices" by some city stores on Wednesdays.

Provincial Shops Regulation Act lists the goods as being in stock-in-trade of certain categories of retail businesses, many of which are required to be closed on Wednesday afternoon by civic bylaw.

Some of these goods are sold out at city retail properties of stages which may be sold Wednesday afternoon are stated are sold illegally on that day, thus harming the business shops which must close Wednesday, argued the spokesman for the Association.

Police officers cannot be expected to carry out such inspections to much effect, the spokesman said, for they have many other more important things called for.

"If regular inspections were made," he said, "the situation would be helped considerably."

A similar complaint was made two weeks ago to the committee by B.C. Retail Hardwareman's Association.

'GOOD NIGHT'S SLEEP' PROVES BIT EXPENSIVE

Carl Page, Martin Hotel, is a sound sleeper.

A sneak thief came into his hotel room and stole $112 from his pants pocket while he slept.

Page had his pants on at the time.

Another hotel resident, J. C. Cranston, Niagara Hotel, told police he awakened early Monday to find a prowler standing over him. The man fled, but when Cranston checked his clothes he found $68 missing.

Curb on Illegal Wednesday Sales

License Inspector Promises Retail Merchants' Ass'n 'Crackdown'

A crackdown on stores which make illegal sales on Wednesdays will be started by Vancouver's license inspectors.

This action was recommended

'Chuckwagon' Got Vancouver Top Publicity

Captain Vancouver Trophy for bringing the most favorable publicity to the city in 1949 has been awarded to James Levick's advertising agency and their "Burns and Company 'Chuckwagon'" radio show.

The award was made by Fred G. Brown, vice-president of the Vancouver Tourist Association at a Board of Trade luncheon Monday.

First honorable mention went to the Canadian Pacific Railway for publicity on inauguration of the CP Airlines Trans-Pacific service.

The Canadian Women's Press Club also received honorable mention as a result of the accounts of its triennial convention that appeared in papers across the country.

The convention was held in Vancouver last summer.

Weary Hunt Goes On for Lost Fliers

Searchers Buck Stormy Weather, Rugged Island Terrain; Still Hopeful

By BILL RYAN
Sun Staff Reporter

ABOARD USCG WHITE HOLLY, Feb. 21 — Weary search crews, who have battled mountains, muskeg, rain, snow and jungle-like forests for days, are still combing Princess Royal Island for five missing B-36 fliers.

It is planned to send reinforcements here within the next day or two to spell off weary teams of Canadians and Americans. Although the U.S. fliers have kept missing for eight days, ever since they bailed from the turning bomber, the search is not yet slackened.

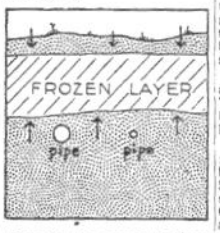

Twelve men survived the ordeal and three of them are now in Canadian group.

Information that might provide a lead for searchers starts in this area.

But wind and rain today are making the search a hard and back-breaking task. Overnight a Moncton-an-hour gale battered the search area. Visibility is poor. Gales to 50 to 60 miles an hour are expected tonight with another storm tomorrow evening after a brief daytime lull.

SURE THREE'S THREE

Capt. Harry L. Barton, who piloted the ill-fated B-36 and is now in Vancouver with crew mates, First-Lieut. Paul Gerhardt and T-Sgt. M. H. Stephens, is still convinced his missing buddies are on Princess Royal. He said the plane was over land when the crew jumped within a space of 15 seconds.

The island is therefore too vast. It is heavily-timbered, precipitous. There are no beaches, sheer rock cliffs front the sea on all sides.

Rarely a day passes when it is not whipped by freezing rain and snow, the terror of bewildered airmen, outright misery to men on the hunt.

Pacific waters about it numb the hand or foot within seconds. Bear tracks are in abundance; deer, rabbit and mountain goat are seen daily.

SEA CERTAIN DEATH

Searchers say the five B-36 crew members unaccounted for may have fallen in the sea. If so, they are dead.

"No one lasts in that water," they may be dead of exposure or injuries on Princess Royal.

But, and this is becoming a long shot, some of them may be clinging to life despite cold and injuries.

So today, as every day for the past five days, ground search crews are inching their way across Princess Royal Island.

Sunday, Vancouver Sun spotter-photographer George Diack and I reached Princess Royal by plane, the first civilian aircraft allowed in the "prohibited area" to give the RCAF. We were the first newsmen to set foot on the island.

ALPINISTS UNCERTAIN

We found skilled mountaineers like Fred Parkes, Charles Jenkins, Herman Genschorek, Adam Melville and Eric Brooks, of B.C. Alpine Club, not so optimistic.

"It's full of ravines and swamps," said Melville and Brooks. "Unless a man walked out you could beat within 30 or 40 feet of where he was lying and never see him."

Planning Board Hits Money Snag

Future of the newly-formed Regional Planning Board for coordinated development of the Lower Mainland and the Fraser Valley may rest on a decision to be made by Vancouver civic officials probably in the next two weeks.

It will most likely depend on Vancouver's willingness to go along with the board's proposed financing plan by which the city would pay the major share of cost.

The board represents 23 municipalities from Vancouver to Hope.

Civic leaders, industries and representatives attended Monday from Abbotsford, Mission, Chilliwack, Maple Ridge, Burnaby, Coquitlam and other communities.

Auxiliary to Meet

NORTH VANCOUVER, Feb. 21 — A meeting of the Ladies Auxiliary to the Fraternal Order of Eagles will be held at 8 p.m. Thursday in St. Alice Hall, 125 West Second Street.

Mumps Leads Diseases Here

Mumps quarantined more school children during January than did any other communicable disease, Superintendent Dr. N. MacCorkindale reported to the Board of School Trustees Monday night.

Total number of cases of mumps was 178. High chicken pox with 130 children; measles, 27; whooping cough, 10; influenza, 9; pneumonia, 7, and scarlet fever, rubella and conjunctivitis, 5 each.

Cases of communicable disease were 127 less than reported for the same period of 1949, Mr. MacCorkindale said.

"LIKE US!" say the two pure bred Afghan hound pups, prizes in the Dog Caricature Contest at city schools, put on by Kiwanis Club of Point Grey in conjunction with their March dog show. They are donated by 11-year-old Wayne Richards, 1744 East First, of Woodland School, and are pictured with Carol Campbell and Gary Ginter of MacKenzie School. Pups have fancy names, El Tajiuen Zora-Kwan, El Tajiuen Meebam.

Not Zeballos Man

Alfred L. Andrews, of Zeballos, says he is not the Andrew Andrews recently convicted in Assize Court here on a charge of indecent assault.

The Alpine Club of Canada, Vancouver chapter, sent five men. The team was led by Fred Parkes, an insurance adjuster in daily life. His group included Charles Jenkins, an insurance broker; Alan Melville, a duplicator; Eric Brooks, a teacher at Lord Byng high school; and Herman Genshorek, a painting contractor and former Canadian Army mountain troops instructor. The five were accompanied by *Daily Province* writer Tom Hazlitt and photographer Bill Cunningham. They whole group flew to the region on an RCAF Lancaster.

Army personnel came from the 129th Heavy Anti-Aircraft Battery, Royal Canadian Artillery, Victoria, B.C.

The five missing men probably died in the icy waters between Gil Island and Princess Royal Island. Some crew in the forward compartment did not wear or carry "Mae West" inflatable life jackets, and nobody wore exposure suits. Everyone was dressed in dry arctic clothing and mukluks instead of the overwater 'wet' clothing. According to the RCAF Search & Rescue Report, Operation Brix, February 1950, "Two of these men were not wearing Mae Wests or dinghys."

Searchers early on found a partially inflated one-man dinghy floating near the shore in the area. This discovery, the initial rescue, and the above calculation as to the probable drop zone for the missing men led the operation to limit the search to one for "washed-up bodies" and a more limited search for the aircraft. After a reasonable length of time, the search was discontinued. A week after the crash fisherman George Reader of the MV *Cape Bathurst* found another partially inflated one-man life raft in Whale Channel.

The four-engined C-54 transport, which took nine of the survivors back to Texas, lost #1 engine over Albuquerque but continued to Fort Worth. The officers would be charged $1.35 per day for room and board while in U.S. military facilities other than Carswell AFB.

Chapter 5: Seek and Destroy in 1954

For three years no one knew what had become of the giant bomber. No wreckage had been sighted in the inland water near the bailout point. A search of the Pacific Ocean in the area where it was set to fly yielded nothing. Although a small oil slick was spotted in the region, it was not thought to be related. The bomber had apparently vanished without a trace.

Then on 2 September 1953, while the RCAF was conducting a search and rescue mission in aid of the lost U.S. millionaire oilman Ellis Hall in his DeHavilland Dove, they spotted the downed bomber far from where anyone had ever thought to look. An immediate call went out to the USAF: "We found your bomber."

Anxious to preserve the secrets of the aircraft, the USAF immediately sent a helicopter to survey the site. Although it did the survey, it was unable to take a ground team in to destroy the aircraft.

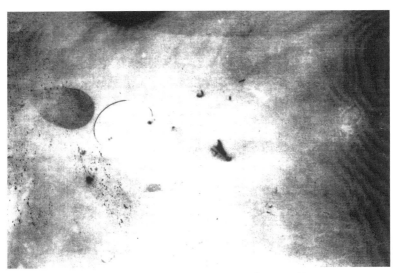

Secret mystery photo from 1953 showing intact aircraft covered in snow.
Credit: U.S. Air Force

Members of the U.S. 1953 expedition using horses to make their way to the crash site. *Credit: U.S. Air Force*

Lt. Paul Gerhart was brought back from the Pacific islands weapons testing operations to fly into the site and look at his bomber. In mid-September 1953, while returning to the United States, the helicopter crash-landed in the Fraser Canyon (Gerhart was not in it when it crashed and nobody died.)

But they now knew the location of the aircraft, and within days a team was sent to the area with orders to reach the aircraft and destroy its most sensitive secrets. In 1953 three expeditions left for the crash site, but none reached the aircraft. All three failed due to distance, snow, weather and the mountainous terrain.

On Monday, 22 September 1953, a team of six U.S. military personnel under the command of Captain Paul Gardella arrived in Smithers seeking to trek to the crash site. Captains Horace Skelton and James Bailey and Sergeants Charles Toulbert and Harold Harvey, and weapons technician Jerry White, all from Fort Worth, Texas, accompanied him.

The team left the following day on packhorses, guided by Jack Lee from Hazelton. Their mission was to salvage certain parts of the bomber as well as personal effects of the crew. Reports at the time indicated that it was thought one of the crew may have stayed with the bomber.

Originally expected to make a nine-day round trip, the expedition endured nineteen days of harsh weather, deep snow and impenetrable terrain. They returned to Hazelton defeated. The next expedition was to fly to a nearby lake and walk to the crash site. That attempt was made during the last week of October when a helicopter was used to airlift the ground party to a small lake north of Hazelton. Deep snow covered the bomber and the helicopter encountered severe icing: the mission was abandoned.

All of the technology in the B-36 was still a closely guarded state secret. The optical and electronic technology for bombing, and the entire electronics suite of jamming and antijamming radios and radars that formed the brain of the aircraft was not to be shared even with the closest allies. And it was certainly not to fall into the hands of the U.S.S.R.

The bomber would have been a great prize to Soviet aircraft designers anxious to learn how the United States had managed to get such range out of an aircraft. Also, the cockpit and bomb bay contained interesting clues about the far superior U.S. nuclear arsenal then being deployed against the U.S.S.R. This was a rational fear on the part of the U.S. military, as during World War II, the U.S.S.R. had impounded three B-29 bombers that landed in the Far East, taken them back to Moscow and totally disassembled and mapped the entire aircraft. These became pattern aircraft used to formulate the similar but distinct Tupolev Tu-4 bomber. Although outwardly identical, no parts were actually interchangeable between the U.S. original and the Soviet knock-off.

Hunter Simpson (far left) and others in 1954. *Credit: U.S. Air Force*

So, with even greater determination, a fourth expedition was organized. And in August 1954 they finally made it. The team gathered in Smithers and picked up local guide Hunter Simpson. Simpson never spoke to anyone about what he did or saw during this expedition and has taken that knowledge to his grave.

Before leaving for the crash site, the team and Simpson drank a lot of coffee at Heggies Diner in Smithers. The team even bothered to steal several coffee mugs from Heggies, two of which were found at their campsite forty-nine years later. One was intact and the second one broken into pieces, but the name Heggies was still as clear as if it was left there yesterday.

Team members Captains James O. Bailey and G. Hayden and Staff-Sergeant J. Stevens, accompanied by Hunter Simpson, were helicoptered up the mountain, with supplies and explosives being airdropped daily. They worked on the aircraft from Saturday, 7 August until Monday, 9 August 1954. Then they were trapped at the site by poor weather until the following Monday afternoon. News reports from the time state that no body was found in the wreckage.

Destruction was centered in the forward crew compartment, cockpit and forward bomb bay containing valuable flight and bombing equipment. Bomb bay number one contained all the items for handling and controlling the atomic bomb and had to be destroyed. So much explosive was used that a pit formed in the rock under where the bomb bay had been. Fires started by the explosions consumed most of the aircraft leaving only occasional puddles of melted metal.

Significant amount of explosive remained scattered around the crash site, and even today small packets can be found in rock crevices. Since 1997 the Canadian Forces has flown in several times to destroy leftover explosives. But it was their 1997 expedition that was most interesting.

Prompted by stories once again circulating in the media, and by complaints by various B.C. residents of a possible nuclear danger in the north, the Canadian military dispatched a team to investigate the possibility of radioactive contamination.

The Department of National Defence, Directorate of Nuclear Safety, sent a radiological survey team into the site on 11 August 1997 for a four-day expedition. The team comprised Lt. Commander David Knight and Chris Thorp of the Nuclear Safety

ABOVE: The successful 1954 expedition prepares to go into the crash site.
Credit: U.S. Air Force.

RIGHT: Members of the 1954 expedition in an aircraft hangar prior to the mission.
Credit: U.S. Air Force.

office at National Defence, and Doug Craig and Doug Davidge of Environment Canada, both of Whitehorse and both longtime interested parties.

They surveyed the entire site and took samples from various locations, wreckage parts and natural features. All of the samples were analyzed by the Atomic Energy Canada Ltd. labs and found to contain no radiation other than the normal background radiation. The only hint of radioactivity was in the cockpit directly below the instrument control panel that had melted in the fire. The instruments at the time of the bomber's manufacturing were painted with a radium paint to make them glow in the dark. This radium paint had also melted and produced a small radiation signature.

There is no evidence of any plutonium or uranium (either natural, depleted or weapons grade) at the crash site.

It is not known what items, if any, the 1954 USAF expedition removed from the site. It is most likely, given the limitation in helicopter technology at the time, that everything was to be destroyed rather than recovered. This accounts for the massive amount of high explosives dropped onto the crash site.

Some have argued that the effort was out of proportion to simply ensure that not one secret remained that could be exploited by a Soviet expedition intent on intelligence about the secret long-range bomber. These people point to the B-36 crashes in Newfoundland that were not subject to the same level of interest or destruction. The reason this was done in B.C. and not in Newfoundland is that the western crash site is totally secluded and could have been exploited by a secret Soviet expedition, something that would have been almost impossible near the U.S. base at Goose Bay. Also, this bomber was fully outfitted to carry and drop nuclear weapons at the time it crashed. There is no evidence this was the case with any B-36s that crashed in Newfoundland. In fact, the only B-36s known to have crashed on the eastern coast were a reconnaissance version and a conventional bomber. The circumstances are so different as to make comparisons useless.

Chapter 6: Expedition 2003 – The Search for Answers

With the first permit for exploration and recovery ever issued by the government, in August 2003 a small team and a camera crew flew to the crash site by helicopter to examine the wreckage, collect artifacts and search for answers.

The quest for a permit was very difficult due to the objections placed in our way by parties who have developed an interest in the wreckage.

One group, identifying themselves as the Broken Arrow Aircraft Society, stated they would not accept a museum expedition to the crash site. Their public letter to the B.C. government opposing our expedition and permit stated that if the permit was granted, they required a BAAS member to accompany us; that all artifacts collected could only be displayed with express written permission of the BAAS; and that once the initial display was finished, all the artifacts would be "returned" to the BAAS.

Of course, the B.C. government informed the BAAS and its president Pierre Cote of Terrace, that as the wreckage was a B.C. Heritage Site and did not belong to the BAAS, and that the BAAS had no legitimate claim to the wreckage, it was impossible to impose such ludicrous conditions upon the expedition. But this did not stop an individual from contacting local and regional helicopter companies in an attempt to stop our expedition. Several companies were told that our expedition was going to steal Native artifacts—a considerable crime in these parts, and one that would scare off any reputable company.

Members of the Terrace-based society first got themselves into trouble with the B.C. government in 1998 for removing artifacts from this site. Various members went to the heritage site and took several objects, which they later displayed on the Internet and at temporary exhibitions. Declassified RCMP records detail many of the BAAS activities and the displeasure of the B. C. government. Lacking any permit to gather the objects, they were in potential violation of the law. When they were informed they had been caught, their response was to set up a so-called museum to house and display the artifacts. Rather than prosecute the men, the B.C. government chose to leave matters rest in the interests of peace. But B.C. never recognized the claim the BAAS made to the artifacts or to the wreckage.

David Suttill of the Ministry of Sustainable Resource Management wrote to me on 20 March 2004, stating, "the original report of looted artifacts being removed from Mt. Kologet in September of 1998 was turned over to the local RCMP in Terrace." He continued that in August of 2001 his office was "informed of a possible infraction of the Heritage Conservation Act (HCA) where Mr. Borutski was alleged to have removed some artifacts from B.C. that originally came from the Mt. Kologet crash site in 1998. This information was immediately turned over to the RCMP in Terrace for investigation."

RCMP records released under the federal Access to Information Act reveal that several items have been specifically recorded as having been removed from the aircraft by named individuals and then handled by a local group. The RCMP records specifically name Doug Davidge and Doug Craig of Whitehorse, Yukon, as having transferred to the Stewart Historical Society several artifacts from the protected heritage crash site on 14 August 1997. These artifacts included one emergency transmitter radio (yellow) with spool radio antenna; one oxygen mask with cylinder; one emergency survival suit (yellow); one leather flight hat with goggles; one pair of U.S. Air Force leather gloves with liners; three assorted first-aid kit items; and two signal flares.

As neither Davidge and Craig nor any of the people from the Stewart Historical Society or the BAAS itself had or has a permit to collect, alter, conserve or deal in these artifacts, the actions recorded by the RCMP constituted a possible violation of the B.C. Heritage Conservation Act (RS Chap. 165, 1979), sections 6.(1) and 6.(2)(a). The penalties laid out in the Act for individuals are a fine of not more than $50,000 and/or two years imprisonment, or for an organization a maximum fine of not more than $1,000,000.

The taking of artifacts has often been done in the open by people proud of their unauthorized activities. The Canadian Press reported on 12 November 1998, that a Terrace-based group had flown into the site by helicopter in the previous months and removed some 20-mm cannon turrets, the aircraft insignia and other items. The removals drew the wrath of the government as the wreckage is classified as a protected historical item. Carl Healey, and other Terrace men who had taken the protected items, tried to atone by setting up the group called the Broken Arrow Aircraft Society as a way of distancing themselves from personal responsibility for the removals. Healey told the media that "It's our history" and "we just wanted to make sure this stuff didn't disappear." Much has already disappeared into private collections.

As a nuclear weapons specialist, I led the team on behalf of the Diefenbunker, Canada's Cold War Museum in Ottawa. James Laird, a B.C. prospector and specialist in the aircraft and incident, wanted to discover how the bomber came to be on the mountain. Dirk Septer, aviation historian and incident specialist also from B.C., searched for human remains and theorized about possible flight paths. The team hoped to discover how the aircraft came to be in its present position, and which way it was flying when it crashed.

Jim Laird and Dirk Septer believe they determined the aircraft was flying in an east-northeast direction when it hit the top of the ridge. As the bailout site is almost directly south, the team expected the aircraft to be heading almost directly north when it crashed. Instead, evidence gathered on the mountain by the two men seems to suggest the aircraft was flying east, ironically at a heading of approximately 075 degrees, when it crashed.

I discovered the pit under what was the bomb bay that had held the atomic bomb. The remains of the atomic bomb shackle and bomb equipment were found. However, I have found no evidence at the crash site or in the declassified records to indicate that the bomb was in the aircraft when it crashed on Mt. Kologet.

A large problem in the way of research is encountered when it is found that many significant artifacts have been looted by treasure-hunters. The "birdcage," a protective case holding a nuclear or lead practice core, and the detonator case are major losses to history.

The birdcage was stolen by a U.S. treasure-hunter from Connecticut. He secretly held the birdcage for several years before becoming frightened that the U.S. government was about to investigate him for holding a nuclear-weapons-related item. He quickly gave the birdcage to the U.S. military's Defense Threat Reduction Agency (DTRA), which initially promised to return it to the proper custody. However, DTRA was asked for the artifact by the U.S. Air Force Museum, and the birdcage began another journey.

The museum would at first not even confirm they had the artifact and stalled all attempts to gain information through legal channels. The birdcage, after spending several months in Dayton, Ohio, was transferred to the Department of Energy office at Sandia National Labs in Albuquerque, New Mexico. As the birdcage was originally the property of the Atomic Energy Commission, now the DoE, Sandia seemed like the appropriate place. It was at first thought that the artifact would be given to the U.S. National Atomic Museum, which is administered by Sandia. That was not the case. The current status of the artifact is unknown, but there is a good chance it will eventually be displayed as a relic of the world's first Broken Arrow.

To date, work to have the looted items placed in proper and responsible custody continues.

(Please see Appendix 6 for a detailed diary of the 2003 expedition.)

Commemorative plaque left by the 2003 expedition. *Credit: Author*

Chapter 7: Mysteries of the First Broken Arrow

Where is the Atomic Bomb?

Testimony from the crew and declassified secret documents from the United States all indicate that prior to bailing out, the Mk-4 atomic bomb was fused to explode at a pre-set altitude after dropping out of the bomb bay and detonate above the water west of Princess Royal Island. The secret 1950 USAF report to a congressional committee, the only declassified statement released so far, says that the bomb was presumably destroyed. This saved all the secrets of this most secret weapon.

A report by Doug Davidge of Environment Canada, Whitehorse, Yukon, of his visit to the site with the CF in August 1997 shows that "the aluminum 'Explosives' box was investigated further by DND personnel. They found it contained 4 of 36 electronic type detonators. The missing 32 detonators are believed to have been used to arm the bomb. The case and documentation identified the detonator components which were intended for use in a Mk IV nuclear device."

The *Fort Worth Star-Telegram* on 16 February 1997, reported their interview with retired Lt. Col. Paul E. Gerhart, the bomber's radar officer who jettisoned the Mk-4 bomb. Gerhart said that, "It was about midnight when I salvoed the bomb, [and] it detonated about 4,000 feet [1,200 m] above the Pacific."

But things were not so clear in Washington. It turned out that once the U.S. Atomic Energy Commission loaned the weapon to the USAF, they (the AEC) lost track of it. It was only when the news of a B-36 crash made headlines in the Washington *Times Herald*, that the AEC became aware of the potential loss. Bill Sheehy of the Joint

Committee on Atomic Energy, which oversaw the AEC, and who had seen the loading of this particular bomb, "became personally as well as officially alarmed" at the possibility that the first loss had occurred.

When Sheehy telephoned USAF Colonel Coiner to enquire as to whether this was the bomber in which the AEC had an interest, the Colonel said that the USAF was not yet certain. The air force then began asking people at Fort Worth whether the aircraft had carried an atomic bomb. Within days it was clear that nobody knew anything, and the USAF was rather embarrassed. Finally, eleven days after the crash, the senators of the Atomic Energy Committee were advised that the bomb had been jettisoned but not detonated to destruction. However, even this came only with a struggle. On 28 February, General Hall of the USAF Legislative and Liaison Section refused to tell the AEC the status of the bomb without a written request. Two weeks later, the senators were told that the bomb had been "exploded while in the air."

The final word was that the senators were not happy with the attitude of the USAF, which was summed up by Sheehy as the air force saying nothing until they were "damn good and ready to tell us what the hell they did with one of our atomic weapons." Unfortunately, there have been no further documents released under the Freedom of Information Act.

Although there is the slimmest possibility the bomb stayed with the aircraft, the bomb shackle shows no evidence of holding a bomb upon impact. So the best documentary, testimonial and physical evidence points to no bomb crashing with the aircraft.

Where is the Nuclear Core?

Although the disposition of the bomb is fairly straightforward, the ultimate status of the nuclear core is a more difficult issue. The core probably remained in the custody of the U.S. Atomic Energy Commission, as its release required the permission of the president of the United States.

According to Major General Thomas D. White in his 17 March 1950 Top Secret report, "The airplane carried an atomic bomb, less nuclear component."

Almost a half century after the incident, several crew members made contradictory statements claiming there indeed was a core on board the aircraft and that it was dropped with the bomb.

Prior to the Korean War, all nuclear cores were under the control of and in the possession of the U.S. Atomic Energy Commission. During the war, President Truman authorized the first cores to be given to Strategic Air Command in April 1951.

Early uranium and plutonium cores were the most expensive and rarest items on earth, and much effort went into their preservation. Each was packed in a protective "birdcage" for transportation. The birdcage would hold the core until it came time to arm the Mk-4 for war use. It also protected the crew from the radiation given off by the core. The early birdcages had parachutes attached. In the case of overwater flights, the birdcage had to be attached to a self-inflating automatic one-man dinghy.

The original birdcage was stolen from the crash site by looters. It is now in the possession of the U.S. Department of Energy, which received it from the U.S. Air Force. The USAF refused to return it to the proper custodians and the museum. The Defense Threat Reduction Agency, responsible for nuclear arms control and verification and nuclear threats to the United States, was given the birdcage by a looter who feared he would be investigated by the FBI for holding a nuclear package carrier. The item was then transferred to the U.S. Air Force, which insisted it not be returned to the museum holding the permit for its acquisition.

The core was probably never on the aircraft. Since the crew left the birdcage on the aircraft, it probably contained nothing but a lead-weight practice core.

In his July 1998 interview done by Don Pyeatt and posted on the Internet, co-pilot Ray Whitfield recalls there was a core onboard, "but it was a 'dummy' core made with lead instead of plutonium."

The Mk-4 bomb in question was one of the first atomic weapons ever to be loaned to the Strategic Air Command from an AEC bomb storage site. The AEC jealously guarded their weapons and probably did not allow the core to be removed from the bunker. Given the sensitivity of control over nuclear weapons, and the fact that the White House had not yet authorized their transfer from the AEC to the military, there was no reason for a nuclear core to be on the bomber.

In 1998 co-pilot Ray Whitfield recalled, "Barry turned the plane out to sea so that we could dump the bomb and the dummy core. As soon as we were safely over the sea we dropped the bomb. It was set to air burst at 3000 feet [400 m]. We were at about 8000 feet [2,400 m] when the bomb exploded so we could see the flash as it exploded."

I continue to press the U.S. Department of Energy to release more records about the incident. To date I have been unsuccessful. The historical division of the DoE stated in October 2004 that they had no additional information on the core. My belief is that this is far too sensitive a topic for the DoE, especially as the U.S. is once again closing files in the U.S. National Archives and is demanding that foreign files on overflights of foreign countries be denied to researchers.

No complete official story on any Broken Arrow has ever been released by the United States. Since this bomb was lost over a foreign country, complete information will probably never be seen.

How Did the Aircraft Get to the Crash Site?

There is no credible explanation of how the aircraft flew from the bailout point (53°02'00" N, 129°10'30" W) 340 km to the crash site (56°03'00" N, 128°32'00" W). I suspect that immediately after the crew bailed out, the bomber flew into a patch of better weather and the ice broke away from the wings. The bomber stabilized and then gained altitude. The autopilot seems to have acted in an erratic manner and may have taken the bomber in various turns.

Some speculate that an autopilot error, combined with improved flying conditions, allowed the bomber to gain altitude and fly several more hours. Another theory is that it is nearly impossible for the aircraft to have made it too far into the mountains without a pilot at the controls.

Some theories indicate the bomber flew for many hours before crashing and flew as far south as Vancouver Island. Such a flight path would have taken at least eight hours for the slow bomber. There is no credible evidence to suggest the bomber was in the air more than the three hours necessary to reach the crash site from the bailout point. However, without knowing the exact time of the crash, we cannot accurately determine the flight time.

One very interesting hypothesis is that the giant bomber flew

Route Map of the doomed B-36 bomber departing Alaska for Texas, but crashing in British Columbia.

SAC emblem.

Eielson AFB

Bombing & Bailout Sites ⊠····· → CRASH

Cape Flattery

Fort Peck

n Francisco
omb Target

Salton Sea

Fort Worth
Home Base

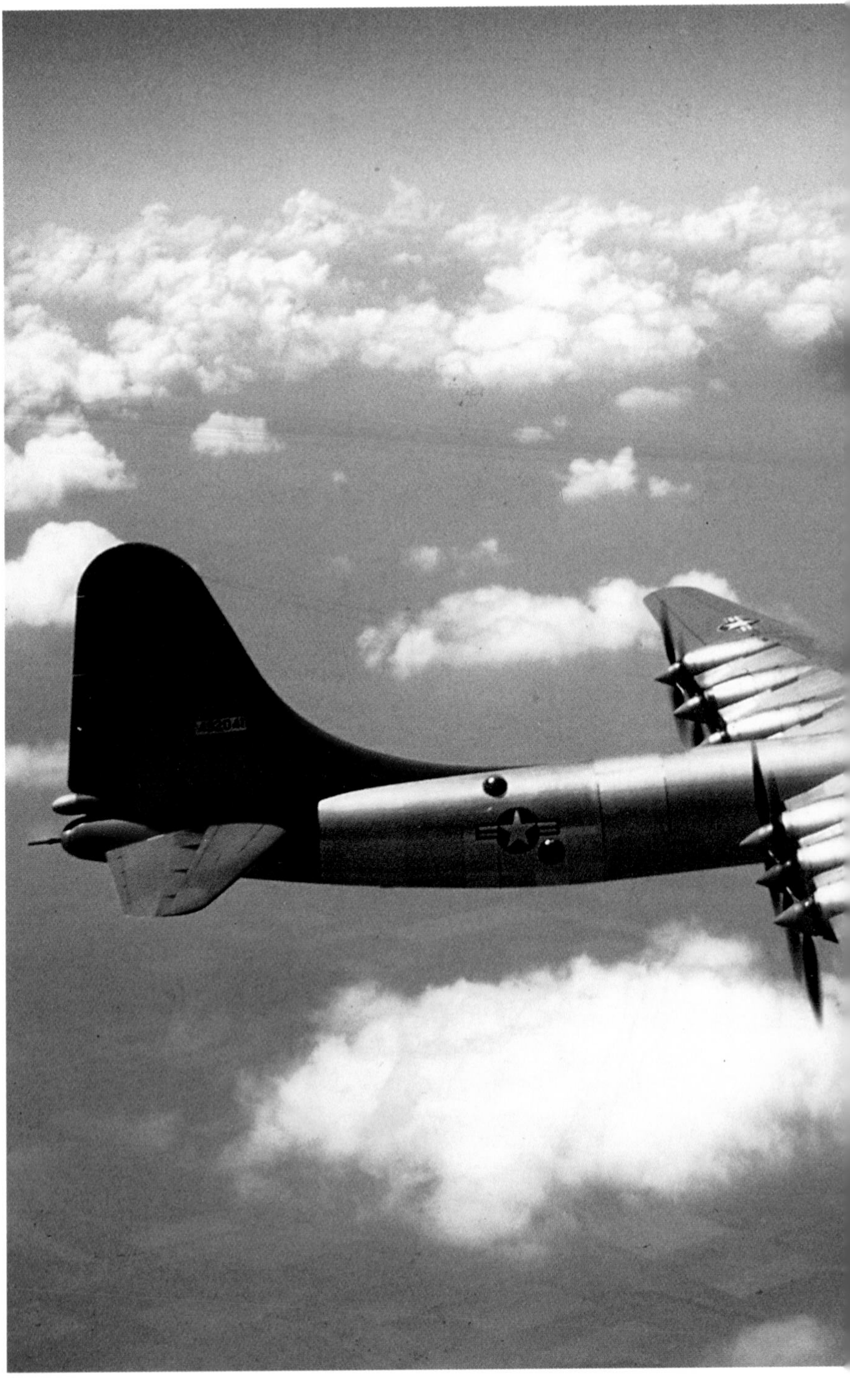

B-36B in flight. *Credit: Convair & U.S. Air Force*

San Francisco bombing target map. *Credit: U.S. Navy*

Full-scale model of the Mk-4 atomic bomb on display at the Diefenbunker Cold War Museum. *Credit: Author*

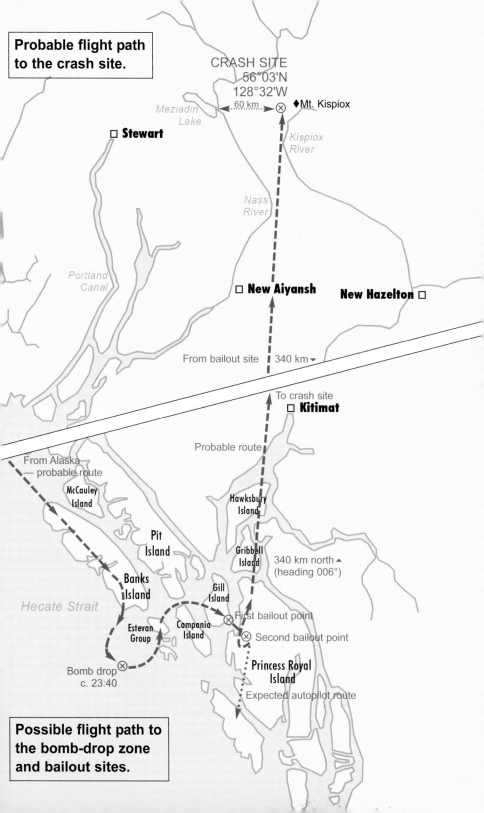

Probable flight path to the crash site.

CRASH SITE
56°03'N
128°32'W

◄·· 60 km ··► ⊗ ♦ Mt. Kispiox

Meziadin Lake

Kispiox River

□ **Stewart**

Nass River

Portland Canal

□ **New Aiyansh**   **New Hazelton** □

From bailout site │ 340 km ▾

To crash site
□ **Kitimat**

Probable route

From Alaska
— probable route

McCauley Island

Hawksbury Island

Pit Island

Gribbell Island

340 km north ▲
(heading 006°)

Banks Island

Gill Island

Hecate Strait

Estevan Group

Campania Island

⊗ First bailout point

⊗ Second bailout point

Bomb drop
c. 23:40 ⊗

Princess Royal Island

⊗·· Expected autopilot route

Possible flight path to the bomb-drop zone and bailout sites.

The explosives suitcase and the birdcage that held the core amongst the wreckage.
Credit: Declassified and released by the RCMP under Access to Information.

The explosives suitcase that held the detonators.
Credit: Declassified and released by the RCMP under Access to Information

The explosives suitcase that held the detonators, open to reveal the security cover.
Credit: Declassified and released by the RCMP under Access to Information

One of four surviving detonators from the accident.
Credit: Declassified and released by the RCMP under Access to Information

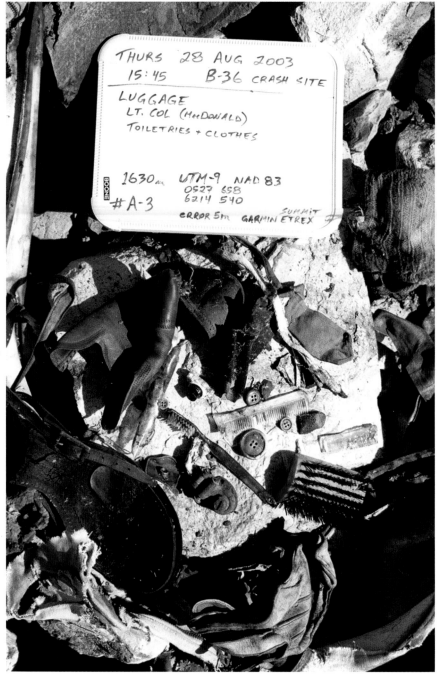

Toiletries kit contents belonging to Lt. Colonel MacDonald found in the wreckage in 2003.
Credit: Author

An unused Mae West life preserver found in the wreckage in 2003. *Credit: Author*

Orange survival kit box discovered torn from a shackle in the rear bomb bay. The food was long gone, but some kit items remained. This item was recovered for preservation. *Credit: Author*

An unused one-man life raft found in the wreckage in 2003. *Credit: author*

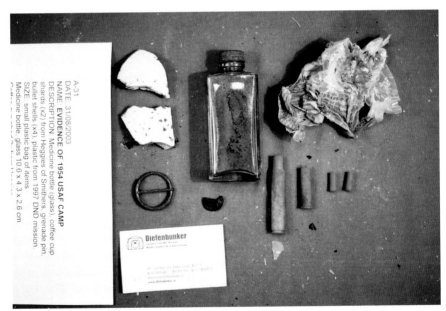

Relics from the 1954 expedition campsite, and plastic from the 1997 DND radiological survey.

Credit: author

Remains of the cockpit. The "greenhouse" canopy frame is clearly visible. *Credit: Author*

Wreckage of the rear crew compartment. *Credit: Author*

Crash site as it appeared in summer 2003. *Credit: Author*

Author with the newly discovered atomic bomb shackle. *Credit: Author*

The newly discovered atomic bomb shackle H-frame face up.
Credit: Author

The newly discovered atomic bomb shackle H-frame face down.
Credit: Author

Close-up of the undamaged bomb shackle locking knuckle in the closed position. Horizontal Pneumatic Bomb Rack, Airplane serial No. 44-92075.
Credit: Author

Daniel V. MacDonald's Lt Color oak leaf cluster rank badge

Replica of the original "birdcage" used to hold the plutonium core of the bomb in the aircraft. *Credit: Author*

Colonel MacDonald's shoulder rank badge found in the rear cabin wreckage. *Credit: Author*

Tools recovered from the cockpit area of the aircraft. *Credit: Author*

Survival kit booklet, matches, candle, and spoon recovered from the bomb bay. *Credit: Author*

The salvo relay box used to transmit the signal to drop the atomic bomb recovered from the H-frame. *Credit: Author*

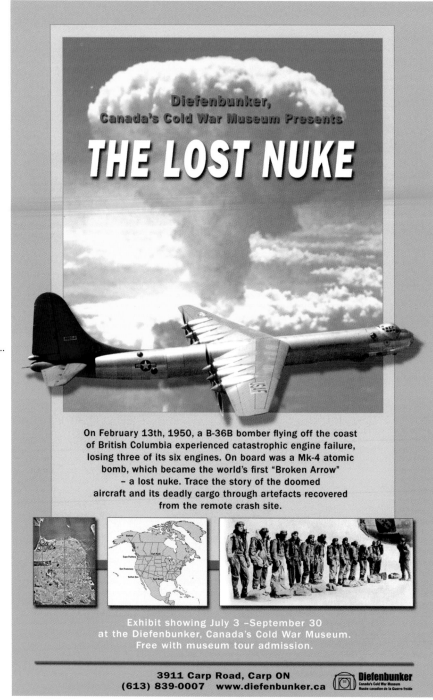

Diefenbunker,
Canada's Cold War Museum Presents

THE LOST NUKE

On February 13th, 1950, a B-36B bomber flying off the coast of British Columbia experienced catastrophic engine failure, losing three of its six engines. On board was a Mk-4 atomic bomb, which became the world's first "Broken Arrow" – a lost nuke. Trace the story of the doomed aircraft and its deadly cargo through artefacts recovered from the remote crash site.

Exhibit showing July 3 –September 30
at the Diefenbunker, Canada's Cold War Museum.
Free with museum tour admission.

3911 Carp Road, Carp ON
(613) 839-0007   www.diefenbunker.ca   **Diefenbunker**
Canada's Cold War Museum
Musée canadien de la Guerre froide

Poster for The Lost Nuke museum permanent display at the Diefenbunker.
Courtesy of Diefenbunker, Canada's Cold War Museum Collection

from the bailout point north to pass over New Aiyansh, north of the Skeena River but only a few minutes flying time south of the crash site. An unconfirmed eyewitness report makes the Reverend Kinley the last person to see the aircraft in flight as it flew over the small settlement around 02:00 a.m. The spotting of the aircraft at this time is crucial to another part of theory that supposes that the aircraft radio continued to transmit until 02:00 when it disappeared from the airwaves.

Now, it is known that before abandoning the aircraft, S/Sgt. Trippodi tied down the radio transmit key so that a steady stream transmission would be broadcast until the plane crashed. The problem with the theory, aside from being unable to get a confirmation about the sighting, is that the radio transmission monitored by the military was found to be in the foreign broadcast band of 4495 kcs and very common in that frequency. It was not on an emergency channel nor did it appear to come from North America. Even if the radio operator did leave the transmit button engaged before bailing, there is no evidence that the transmissions were heard by anyone.

Without access to the full records held by the U.S. Air Force and the U.S. Department of Energy, we shall never know the complete truth.

A Few Words About an Alternate Theory

There are several conspiracy theories surrounding this incident. That is hardly a surprise, given that it involves a lost atomic bomb, a giant bomber missing for three years and five men missing to this day.

The main problem with the theories advanced by the conspiracy aficionados is that they have never been able to explain how a nuclear core came to be on the aircraft. Since it has been proven through documentation and eyewitnesses that no cores were released to the U.S. military until the spring of 1951, asserting that a nuclear core was onboard requires a great leap of faith. In fact, it cuts to the heart of the constitutional question of presidential authority and would have meant that the U.S. military had somehow stolen a core or had conspired with the U.S. Atomic Energy Commission to illegally obtain a core without presidential authority.

James Laird, who was on the expedition to the crash site in

August 2003, has advanced one interesting and coherent but totally unprovable theory. His writings are now part of the collection of artifacts and materials associated with the *Lost Nuke* documentary kept at the Diefenbunker Museum near Ottawa and are viewable by the interested public upon application.

In Laird's view, the Mk-4 atomic bomb was dropped out of the aircraft and conventionally detonated prior to the bailout of the crew. However, he suggests the plutonium core was in the birdcage and onboard the aircraft. Laird notes that of the last three men on the aircraft, only Schreier was authorized to handle the nuclear material. The men are thus thought to have decided to leave Schreier onboard and allow him to attempt to fly the crashing aircraft and plutonium back to Alaska.

The theory never explains how Schreier, flying a crippled and iced-up aircraft that required several flight crew, managed to not only fly the airplane by himself but also cause the ice to break off and the aircraft to gain altitude. Schreier would have had to fly the aircraft from the pilot position as well as switch back and forth with the engineer positions in order to transfer fuel to stabilize the aircraft, something the two trained engineers had been unable to do prior to bailout. But there is no reasonable explanation for this event.

Under this theory, Schreier would then have had to re-engage the autopilot in order to move the birdcage and fuse suitcase to the safer rear compartment. Then, for an unexplained reason, he would have had to try to find a place to land outside of Alaska. Laird suggests that Schreier flew over both Terrace and New Aiyansh while simultaneously navigating, piloting the aircraft, moving cargo to the rear compartment and doing the job of the engineers. And although no eyewitness testimony has ever been verified or even shown to be even somewhat reliable, the theory at this point is based on the notion that the aircraft was positively identified by a priest in New Aiyansh at 1:45 in the morning. Schreier, presumably, would now had to have been flying to the old airstrip at Woodcock. Unable to find a place to land, Laird suggests that Schreier began to fly east through the Kispiox where the giant bomber gently crashed on the deep snow at about 3:00 a.m.

The timing of the crash is important to the theory, as it is suggested that a clear radio signal was heard from the aircraft all that time, only ceasing at exactly 2:05. However, this has never been verified, and it was known that the aircraft radio operator was unable to transmit beyond the range of the accompanying bomber.

Although highly unlikely to be true, Laird's theory is important as it seeks to explain the inexplicable. No one has ever proven how #92075 came to be on a mountain in northern British Columbia. It remains one of the great mysteries of the Cold War.

Chapter 8: More Nuclear Accidents

Early in the nuclear age, the U.S. military developed a code language for speaking about incidents and accidents involving nuclear weapons. For quick reference the military would be able to use the following code words in describing an incident:

Nucflash: This category of incident or accident signifies a situation in which a detonation or unauthorized incident could create the risk of nuclear war between the U.S.A. and U.S.S.R./Russia.

Broken Arrow: The Broken Arrow code indicates that a nuclear weapon is in danger of exploding or that it has exploded or been lost. This does not refer to detonations that carry the risk of starting a war. It does cover the theft, seizure or intentional jettisoning of nuclear weapons or critical components.

Bent Spear: This category covers incidents and accidents in which a nuclear weapon has been damaged and will need repair or the replacement of major components. There is no risk of detonation. It also covers incidents in which there is a political risk of adverse public reaction or the inadvertent release of information to the public.

Dull Sword: This is the lowest level of nuclear incident involving a nuclear weapon or nuclear weapon system. These are nonsignificant incidents that could impair the operational capability of the weapon or weapon system but are not capable of causing a detonation.

Since 1950 there have been hundreds of nuclear weapons accidents. Between 1950 and 1968 alone, at least 1,250 U.S. nuclear weapons were involved in accidents or incidents of varying severity, including 272 that crashed or fell to the ground and in many cases resulted in high explosive detonations. Of these 272 weapons, forty-one bombs or warheads were aboard aircraft that crashed and twenty-four weapons were jettisoned or inadvertently released from aircraft or ships.

The most famous nuclear weapons accident happened in 1966 when a U.S. Air Force B-52 bomber collided with another aircraft and dropped four thermonuclear weapons near the Spanish town of Palomares. Two of the bombs broke apart and released radioactive plutonium, and two bombs were lost in the sea beside the town. It took three months to recover the last bomb.

Greenpeace identified 383 nuclear weapons involved in U.S. Navy incidents alone between 1965 and 1977. A U.S. government study said that the U.S. Navy reported 233 incidents involving nuclear weapons between 1965 and 1983.

The Bombing of Riviere du Loup

Nine months after the B-36 crash in B.C., another U.S. bomber lost an atomic bomb in Canada. It was their fifth Broken Arrow and the second in Canada. On 10 November 1950, the lead B-50A bomber lost power in two of its four engines and dropped its atomic bomb over the St. Lawrence River in Quebec.

In a memo to Secretary of State for External Affairs Lester Pearson, Canadian Ambassador Hume Wrong wrote on 2 December 1950, "It was during transportation of these weapons to the United States that the incident occurred over the St. Lawrence River in which one of the bombs had to be jettisoned and detonated."

In the summer of 1950, special arrangements were made for the temporary stationing of a U.S. Air Force's Strategic Air Command Bombardment Group at Royal Canadian Air Force Station Goose Bay, for a six-week period of training. Given that the Korean War had begun, and that the USAF had deployed a Wing of B-50 bombers to Europe due to the tensions there, this was clearly more than an exercise. SAC Headquarters picked the 43rd Bombardment Group/43rd Bombardment Wing for the assignment.

Back in August 1950 USAF/SAC also sought high-level, secret permission to bring eleven "special weapons" (atomic bombs) to the Goose Bay deployment site. This was described as an action brought about by the current period of emergency, which also saw atomic bombs deployed to Great Britain. Prime Minister Louis St. Laurent had been informed of the United State's request by RCAF Air Marshal Curtis. Strategic Air Command had chosen Curtis as the contact man in Canada and relied on him to deal with the prime minister and military staff. The PM limited his permission to the six-week deployment period.

In Ottawa, the PM and Air Marshal Curtis were in the know; and at External Affairs, the secretary of state and under-secretary of state as well as a select few men had this knowledge. Only three people at the Canadian Embassy in Washington knew of the plans, and the chairman of the joint staff was not one of them. The full cabinet heard nothing of the deployment at all until 18 August 1950, when the chief of the air staff told them, "It seemed probable that a request would be forthcoming for permission to move a group of medium bombers and two squadrons of tankers to Goose Bay. It was not clear exactly what purpose the units were to serve." In reply, Minister of National Defence Brooke Claxton stated, "In connection with the U.S. request, it might be desirable to get further information, although there should be no hesitation about granting any reasonable request." The cabinet then agreed to instruct DND to seek clarification of the request. Goose Bay is then not discussed again until 25 October 1950, when the cabinet briefly talks about the possible expansion of facilities at the station. No mention is ever made of atomic weapons or of the accident.

Before the wing moved, intricate preparations took place. The secret history of the 64th Bombardment Squadron states that on 23 August 1950, "Lieutenant Hawke departed for the maneuver area via a devious route. All Special Weapons personnel were briefed by Captain Ferko, Group Special Weapons Officer. Second Lieutenants Richard C. Henry, Robert A. Wilke, and Stewart V. Spragins, all reported for duty." These special weapons personnel, all pilots, then prepared for the deployment.

The 43rd Bomb Group acted in compliance with Fifteenth Air Force Operations Order 18-50 of 3 August 1950 and prepared to move three bomber squadrons of fifteen B-50 aircraft each to Goose

Bay and two refueling squadrons of nineteen KB-29 aircraft each to Harmon Air Base. Originally, five bombers were to fly to Goose Bay each day. Along the way, a number of the bombers would pick up conventional weapons at Gray Air Force Base for carriage to Goose Bay.

The 43rd Bombardment Wing began its move to Goose Bay on 26 August and was in place by 30 August 1950. Goose Bay Station records show that on the day of 27 August, forty-three bombers arrived at the Goose. However, engine failures caused some aircraft to be delayed, and the final bomber arrived on 11 September. At the beginning of September 1950, the wing had forty-four B-50 bombers on inventory, with forty-three deployed to Goose Bay. Counting the tankers as well, they had deployed more than seventy-five aircraft. The Wing also had 616 officers and 3,560 men living in tents scattered about the grounds at the Goose. And deep in the forest they had eleven atomic bombs.

A number of aircraft had clearly brought atomic bombs to Goose Bay. The secret history of the Security Section of the 43rd Bombardment Wing notes:

> Upon arrival at destination, bomb carriers were met by cleared Air Police security guards...After classified units were unloaded from bomb carriers guards accompanied units from aircraft to Restricted Storage Area and aircraft were declassified. Units were stored in a forest, on gravel roads, approximately four miles from the base proper. Units were stored 300 feet [100 m] apart and 1500 feet [460 m] from nearest well-traveled road. Each unit was guarded 24 hours a day...A Corporal of the Guard was posted at the barricaded entrance to the Storage Area.
>
> The Assembly Area was approximately two and one-half miles from Storage Area. Two roving foot patrols were utilized around the Assembly Building to double check SAC Identification Passes and for radiological safety enforcement.

The personnel caring for the precious few atomic bombs had brought sixty-one different types of handling equipment with them, and their assembly and technical buildings contained another 141 pieces of electrical testing equipment.

Within days of their arrival at Goose Bay, the 43rd Bomb Wing

B-50 aircraft lined up at Goose Bay Air Base, Newfoundland, autumn 1950.
Credit: U.S. Air Force via author

was already in operation. On September 6, they flew six "Big Stick" practice strategic bombing missions, probably in the direction of Europe. During one exercise, a B-50 crashed off the end of the runway. Fortunately, it was unarmed.

On 28 September, USAF/SAC requested permission from the Canadian government for the urgent construction of atomic bomb storage bunkers at Goose Bay, as there were absolutely no facilities of any kind there. At that time, SAC was already storing eleven atomic bombs out in the bush a short drive from the base. The Canadian ambassador to the U.S. commented to the under-secretary of state for External Affairs that the USAF did "not envisage the storage of special weapons at Goose Bay until the additional construction there is available." In fact, the 43rd already had the atomic weapons with them, storage bunkers or no storage bunkers.

As this was only a temporary deployment, and as winter was beginning to set in to the region, the Wing prepared to return all its men and equipment to the warmth of the southwest U.S.A. It was also time to return the special weapons to their home in the States. The secret history of the 43rd Bombardment Wing notes that on 9

November 1950, a "Classified mission [was] flown to Goose Bay, Labrador." It also noted that it happened the day before; on 8 November 1950, "18 B-50 aircraft departed for Harmon Air Force Base and Goose Bay, Labrador, to participate in a classified maneuver ordered by Headquarters Strategic Air Command." They flew under Wing Operation Order 20-50, and returned to Davis-Monthan AFB (DMAFB) on 11 and 12 November.

The Goose Bay records note that seventeen B-50s arrived on November 10 for a western flight to the U.S.A. "It was during transportation of these weapons to the United States that the incident occurred over the St. Lawrence River in which one of the bombs had to be jettisoned and detonated owing to engine trouble in one of the transporting aircraft."

On 10 November 1950, a Strategic Air Command 43rd Bomb Group B-50 bomber on its way from Goose Bay to DMAFB, dropped an atomic bomb in the middle of the St. Lawrence River.

On the return trip of this classified mission, four bombers experienced engine troubles: one from the 63rd Bombardment Squadron and three from the 64th Bombardment Squadron. Details of the incidents show that only one aircraft had a failure in two of its four engines. B-50 #46-038 had valve problems, possibly due to icing, on its way from Goose Bay to Davis-Monthan and landed in Maine on 10 November. The aircraft had been flying at an altitude of between 3,000 and 4,500 meters (10,000 and 15,000 ft.). The engines failed, whether from icing alone or from valve failures brought about by icing. It was, however, able to fly on to Limestone Air Force Base in Maine for repairs. This bomber, and the three others, returned to DMAFB by mid-November.

The other bombers from the 64th Bombardment Squadron to experience problems were #46-031, which blew out an intake manifold on one engine, and bomber #46-026, which developed a bad cylinder on one engine. All three stopped at Limestone Air Force Base in Maine for repairs. The trio returned to DMAFB by mid-November. B-50 #46-047A of the 63rd Bombardment Squadron had an oil leak due to a faulty oil seal on the propeller shaft of engine #2 on its way from Goose Bay to DMAFB and also landed at Limestone AFB that day. It flew on to DMAFB on November 13. Less than week later, on 16 November, this twice-unlucky aircraft would crash and burn.

This was no ordinary bomber crew: they were what SAC Commander Curtis LeMay called a "lead select crew," and were appropriately high ranked. Crew S-020 of eleven men flew #46-038 that cold, icy day. The Aircraft Commander, Major Charles F. Gove, acted as pilot that day; the all-important position of the bombardier was filled by Major Newton Brown. Major Donald Barret was the navigator and Major Bruce Knutson the radar observer. In addition, there were the pilot, flight engineer, radio operator and four gunners. Wing Deputy Commander Lt. Colonel Moore was also present, acting as aircraft commander, as this bomber was the lead aircraft on the mission to return the special weapons to the United States.

As they approached the St. Lawrence River their first engine failed. Soon a second engine, on the other wing, began to backfire and was throttled back. Fully loaded with fuel and the atomic bomb, the aircraft had little hope of making it to a U.S. base, and USAF/SAC Standard Operating Procedure called for the bomb to be dropped. The fuses were to be set to detonate the bomb at 1,200 meters above the water. After checking the river for shipping both visually and with radar, and on consultation with the aircraft commander and pilot, Major Brown released the bomb from the bomb bay when B-50 #46-038 had made its way out over the center of the St. Lawrence River, not far from Riviere du Loup, Quebec.

The 2,200 kilograms (4,850 lb.) of high explosive used to implode the fissile material in the 5-tonne (10,900-lb.) bomb detonated at 775 meters (850 yd.) above the surface of the river, causing great alarm to the people of St. Andre de Kamouraska, St. Simeon and Pointe au Persil on both sides of the river. The fission package was not in the bomb casing, so there was no chance of a nuclear detonation. It was this in-flight insertion (IFI) feature that saved the middle of the St. Lawrence from being irradiated. The plutonium or uranium core was always carried separately from the bomb and only inserted prior to approaching the target. It was not on board the aircraft that day.

The bomber would proceed to Limestone Air Force Base at Limestone, Maine, not far south of the Canadian border. Although not in the best condition for flight, the aircraft was serviceable and should have recovered safely. However, the pilot for the landing dropped the aircraft onto the runway with such force that the main

DEFINITION OF AN ACCIDENT

An "accident involving nuclear weapons" is defined as

- An unexpected event involving nuclear weapons or nuclear weapons components that results in any of the following:

--Accidental or unauthorized launching, firing, or use, by U.S. forces or supported allied forces, of a nuclear-capable weapon system which could create the risk of an outbreak of war.

--Nuclear detonation.

--Non-nuclear detonation or burning of a nuclear weapon or radioactive weapon component, including a fully assembled nuclear weapon, an unassembled nuclear weapon, or a radioactive nuclear weapon component.

--Radioactive contamination.

--Seizure, theft, or loss of a nuclear weapon or radioactive nuclear weapon component, including jettisoning.

--Public hazard, actual or implied.

February 13, 1950 / B-36 / Pacific Ocean, off Coast of British Columbia

The B-36 was enroute from Eilson AFB to Carswell AFB on a simulated combat profile mission. The weapon aboard the aircraft had a dummy capsule installed. After six hours of flight, the aircraft developed serious mechanical difficulties, making it necessary to shut down three engines. The aircraft was at 12,000 feet altitude. Icing conditions complicated the emergency and level flight could not be maintained. The aircraft headed out over the Pacific Ocean and dropped the weapon from 8,000 feet. A bright flash occurred on impact, followed by a sound and shock wave. Only the weapon's high explosive material detonated. The aircraft was then flown over Princess Royal Island where the crew bailed out. The aircraft wreckage was later found on Vancouver Island.   * 1

J - 3

landing gear was almost driven up through the wings. Nobody was injured, and the crew was immediately debriefed on the classified aspects of the incident.

The news would spread quickly of a massive explosion in the St. Lawrence, and the USAF promptly issued a cover story. As it was told in the *Montreal Gazette* on 11 November, a SAC four-engined B-50 bomber on a routine training flight from Goose Bay to Tucson, Arizona, jettisoned a load of 220-kilogram (500-lb.) practice bombs into the St. Lawrence River after experiencing engine trouble. The article noted that the explosion had taken place between the Quebec river communities of Port-au-Persil and St-Simon to the north, and Kamouraska and St. Andre to the south. Residents reported thinking that in that time of international tensions, this was a bombing attack. The cover story did not fool External Affairs and talks quickly began as the U.S. sought to mollify the Canadians.

Despite the early appalling accident record, thousands of nuclear weapons would transit over Canada in bombers and transporters and through Canadian waters in ships and submarines in the subsequent decades.

Appendix 1: Description of the Accident

Following is a partial description of the accident from the U.S. Air Force Accident Board of Inquiry, Carswell AFB, February 1950.

The aircraft was enroute from Eielson Air Force Base, Alaska, to its home station, Carswell Air Force Base, Ft Worth, Texas, on a training mission simulating the profile of an actual combat mission including night and high-altitude flying. The aircraft commander, pilot, flight engineer, and crew were thoroughly experienced in the aircraft and its emergency procedures.

A heavy load take-off was made at 0027Z, 14 February 1950, with a ground temperature of –27 degrees F. The aircraft had been on the ground at Eielson from 13 2108Z [meaning 13 Feb, 21:08 Zulu (GMT)], three hours and nineteen minutes, and the temperature on landing was –40 degrees F. Minor maintenance, including retorquing of hose clamps on #3 and #4 engines to stop fuel leaks, had been accomplished on the ground, and the aircraft took off in good mechanical condition except for radar. The aircraft crew members worked on the radar for about two hours after take-off before completing repairs. Take-off required considerable airspeed, full "nose-up" elevator trim, and stick pulled all the way back to get off the ground. Aircraft left the ground between 135–140 mph.

Weather was good before suspected icing conditions were reached with aircraft flying in the clear and not in clouds. The crew was having trouble making voice position reports on the flight and was required to relay its position at the required check points through B-36 2083.

At about 14 0725Z when flight altitude was 12,000 feet and outside air temperature –17 degrees C uncorrected, light turbulence was encountered. The radar operator reported no thunderstorms in the area but reported what appeared to be snow storms to the right and in the immediate vicinity. Then the crew heard what appeared

#1. As soon as the scanner called in - fire in #1 coming out around the airplug, the engineer feathered it and turned the manual switch to stop it. The scanner called fire in #2, so he feathered that one and between the fire in #1 and 2 the engineers changed seats, the 2d engineer had been in the seat, well, the first engineer asked the scanner where the fire was coming from - and he said from the top of the air plug, so he was about to get things settled down when the right scanner called fire in #5, so he feathered that one, and by that time we were losing altitude quite rapidly in excess of 500 feet a minute and I asked the Radar Operator to give me a heading to take me out over the water. We kept our rapid rate of descent and we got out over the water just about 9,000 feet and the co-pilot ran the bomb bay doors and hit the salvo switch and at first nothing happened, so he hit it again and this time it opened. The radar operator gave me a heading to take me back over land the engineer gave me emergency power to try to hold our altitude. We still descended quite rapidly and by the time we got over land we were at 5,000 feet. So, I rang the alarm bell, and told them to leave.

General ATKINSON: You were at about 5,000 feet above the terrain.(Indicated)

Captain BARRY: 5000 feet indicated above sea level. The radar operator told me that there was terrain which in a few places ran up to 3500 feet and that is one reason I wanted them out.

General ATKINSON: Preparing to go back, and you just indicated ... back when you were flying at 12,000 feet in the ... And, tell me ... in words what preparatory measures you took when you started in the overcast.

Captain BARRY: Well, I didn't have time to take any preparatory measures, because I didn't see any overcast.

4

to be hail beating against the aircraft. The aircraft lost ten miles per hour airspeed. A slight erratic prop surge was experienced on all props. They did not seem to control too well automatically, and RPM was increased to 2300 but no ice was heard to come off the props. The aircraft commander, deciding that icing conditions were being encountered, gave the order to climb. Previous to this, and during daylight hours, frost was seen to accumulate on the leading edge of the wings. At about this time ice was noticed on the antenna by the flight engineer. Also, gunners reported the forward part of blisters were iced over on the outside. As a result of the frost on wings, the wing and tail anti-icing were operated every thirty to forty-five minutes for about twenty-five-minute periods at maximum temperatures from take-off.

All flight engineer instruments were registering normally, with carburator air temperature between 25 degrees to 30 degrees C and CHT's [Cylinder Head Temperature] between 228 degrees and 230 degrees C, except for #1 engine fuel flow. At first cruise power at 10,000 feet this engine was found to be running too rich with fuel flow 150 pounds per hour above normal, CHT (cylinder head temp) 200 degrees C, and torque pressure 25 PSI low. With some difficulty the fuel flows on this engine was reduced to 40 pounds per hour above normal by manual leaning and the torque and CHT came up to normal.

Climb power of 2650 BHP [British Horse Power], 2550 RPM, was applied and normal rate of climb and airspeed (155) was obtained. After reaching about 14,000 feet to 14,500 feet the rate of climb and airspeed began to drop off. An erratic increase in fuel flow with a corresponding decrease in torque and a surging of the propellers was noted by the flight engineer. Intercoolers had been closed during the entire flight. Carburator pre-heat was applied for the first time but found to be disconnected. The aircraft leveled off at 15,000 feet pressure altitude because of inability to climb further. CAT [carb air temp] was [about] 25 degrees to 35 degrees C on all engines; CHT was 225 degrees to 232 degrees C; and outside air temperature was about -19 degrees C uncorrected. Climb power was retained in an effort to build up the airspeed. The maximum airspeed that was obtained in level flight with climb power was 165.

Prop surging was so bad that they were uncontrollable in automatic. They were placed in the fixed position where control was better, but surging continued.

The left scanner then reported #1 engine afire with about 4 ft blue flames coming from around the air plug. #1 was immediately feathered and climb power was reduced to cruise power on the other five engines. Fuel flow increased to 400 to 500 pounds above normal, and torque pressure dropped slightly again to 145 to 160 PSI on all engines. Manual leaning to the extent considered safe by the flight engineer was attempted without running the danger of going into what the flight engineer considered to be too close to idle cut off; however, manual leaning of the mixture caused the fuel flow to drop to only about 100 pounds per hour.

The left scanner then reported #2 afire in the same manner, and it was immediately feathered. Sparks were reported coming from #2 after feathering. The aircraft was losing altitude rapidly. Approximately 1½ minutes later #5 was reported on fire and immediately feathered. The fire warning lights did not come on in any instance, although they tested OK on the test circuit. The reported fires went out on all engines when they were feathered.

Emergency power was applied to the remaining three engines, but the torque pressure did not increase. The rate of descent was slowed down to about 100 feet per minute with the airspeed indicating about 135 mph. At this point the aircraft weighed about 270,000 pounds.

Because of darkness, the cloud condition and the amount of ice on the airfoils were not visible. Severe rime icing was forecast in this area and altitude. The crew bailed out from about 5,000 feet into rain when the radar operator reported that they were over land. Time of bail-out was about 0805Z 14 February 1950 in the vicinity of Princess Royal Island, British Columbia.

This Board did not investigate the search and rescue and the classified equipment aspects of this accident. If considered necessary, it is believed that these additional investigations should be conducted by the Commanding General, 7th Bomb Wing, Carswell Air Force Base, Fort Worth, Texas.

Conclusions

It is concluded that:

1. While flying on instruments, in icing conditions, climbing at rated power from 12,000 feet, reduced ability to climb

occurred at approximately 14,000 feet; that this condition was brought about by some loss of power and probably by ice on the air foils; (propellers, wings, tail surfaces), that aircraft could not climb above 15,000 feet at rated climb power settings; that while crew was attempting to build up airspeed at this altitude in level flight still using rated climb power fire developed in #1 engine and was immediately feathered; that power was then reduced on other five engines; that #2 and #5 engines, in that order, developed similar fires and were feathered in a very short period of time; that emergency power was applied to remaining engines; however, aircraft could not maintain level flight, that at approximately 5,000 feet the crew executed a successful bail-out of all crew members.

2. The flight crew on B-36 #44-92075 was competent and that the accident did not occur as a result of any incompetency or lack of good judgment on the part of any crew member.

3. The aircraft, before take-off at Eielson Air Force Base, was in good mechanical condition for the type of mission to be flown and that there is no reason to believe it would not operate satisfactorily throughout the mission.

4. From the testimony given by several crews, Air Force engineers and civilian technicians, no fully established procedures are in evidence on the proper and best methods to combat ice, (carburator, venturi icing and intercooling icing in passages and bleeds), both internally and externally, on the B-36 airplane. Further, that combat crew methods and techniques vary as a result of this lack of established procedures and that this is primarily due to the little known reactions of this aircraft to icing conditions, particularly carburator ice.

5. Not all aircraft are equipped with Aldis lamps and not all crew members are familiar with the advantages to be gained in having the Aldis lamp aboard the aircraft so there may be available a positive means to determine at night when ice is forming on wings and tail surfaces.

6. Although exhaust system failure may have occurred in one or more engines, failure of the exhaust system is not believed to be a contributing factor in this accident.

7. After interrogation of other crews, engine fires of a similar nature have occurred numerous times resulting in some instances in extreme emergency conditions. Further, that this board believes the Air Force has been extremely fortunate that there have been no previous serious accidents traceable to this condition. It is believed that excellent crew discipline and superior pilot technique, plus the fact that the aircraft were operating in the ZI where emergency fields are available, have been the major factors in averting serious accidents.

8. Certain materiel deficiencies directly affecting safety of flight in B-36 aircraft are in evidence and must be corrected before full employment of this type aircraft can be utilized in the performance of its primary mission. These include carburation, exhaust systems, and propeller anti-icing.

9. It is questionable as to whether supervisory personnel and flight crews were sufficiently impressed with the severity of icing conditions, which is frequently encountered along the coast of Alaska. This area is known to frequently contain severe icing and turbulence during storm periods far beyond the severity normally encountered in the Zone of the Interior [continental United States].

10. Considering that the B-36 aircraft is unproved in its capability to cope with severe icing conditions, and the fact that severe icing conditions were forecast, there is reason to believe that more emphasis should have been placed on the importance of avoiding icing conditions. This should have been accomplished by command action rather than through a staff Weather Officer.

Appendix 2: Search Reports

*The following is the RCAF Operation BRIX Daily Search Summary,
which has been truncated for clarity.*

Searchmaster F/L D.G. Bell-Irving

Op Brix Daily Search Summary, 14 February

Aircraft 650 searched 150 square miles on the Southwest side of
Calvert Island using square search at 300 feet with half mile visibility. A fair coverage was obtained despite heavy rain. The area along
the airway half way to Sandspit was searched from 300 feet with
seven scanners. Dakota 676 searched the area NE of Port Hardy
with indefinite results because of heavy rain. Beechcraft 105 made
no search beyond Port Hardy because of heavy rain which made forward observation nil. Norseman 370 searched the coastline from
Comox to Port Hardy with no results. USAF aircraft based at
McChord and Spokane made no search due to unfavourable weather. NAS Whidbey Island reported search operations by Fairwing 4
aircraft. The area assigned was bounded by the lines joining 52N
131W, 53N 131W, 53N 129W and 52N 128W. The first flight of
four P2V aircraft obtained complete coverage of Caamano Sound
and the southern tip of Estevan and Capania Islands, with the exception of the areas above 500 feet on Capania or on the mainland in
the southeast section of the search area. With the exception of the
higher ground 50 percent of Moresby Island was covered. The second group of Fairwing 4 aircraft from NAS Whidbey Island
searched the same area as the first group with the same coverage. An
oil slick one mile long and 50 to 70 feet wide with the centre at
5226N and 12937W was found. Results from all other areas
searched were negative. Flying time for 12 Group aircraft was 18
hours 55 minutes. One PBY with seven pair eyes and 2JRF with 3

pair of eyes searched the following: 60% of Cape St. James to Cape Scott 10 miles wide; 30% of the shoreline and coastal islands Estevan to Triple Island; 50% of bays and inlets of east and west coast Queen Charlotte Island south of Sandspit; 10% of water sear between Cape St. James and Amber 1 to 30 miles southeast; 20% of Principe Channel and the west and south shoreline of Banks Island Igden Channel, Portland Inlet, Nass Bay; and 10% of north side of Nass River and Nass Bay to Aiyansh four miles inland. Height 500–100 feet with 1 to 3 miles visibility in all areas except north Nass River where heights 1000–7500 feet were flown. Total search time — 27 hours and four minutes.

Op Brix Daily Search Summary, 15 February

Plan for the 15th was to continue search of all areas covered 14 Feb north of 53 degrees latitude including water area. The USCG assignments for the 15th were the area between 52N and 53N to be covered by 8 Navy P2V planes from NAS Whidbey. Two B-17s and one SA10/Catalina from Air Rescue Service McChord to cover water areas between latitudes 51 and 52 north. A Coast Guard JRF to cover the islands and coastal area adjacent to 128W between latitude 52 and 52 North. A Coast Guard PBY to cover islands on east side Queen Charlotte Sound and Hecate Strait.

At 1300 PST fish boat "Cape Perry" sighted smoke on Princess Royal Island and picked up two survivors of the B-36 crash. This was passed to 12 Group HQ via Northwest Telephones. This information was passed to all concerned and two RCAF Cansos were despatched to area from Port Hardy. Further information was received from the fish boat "Cape Perry" that he was picking up survivors all along Princess Royal Island, also that there was one airman hanging by his parachute on the side of a cliff beside a small lake two or three miles inland from the west coast of Princess Royal Island. Dakota 676 was despatched with para-rescue personnel to the scene. Canso 11067 and 11015 reported that a Coast Guard PBY picked up survivors and airlifted them to Port Hardy. Dakota 676 after an extensive search of the area was unable to locate the injured airman on cliff. At 1630 HMCS *Cayuga* put ground search personnel ashore. A civilian alpine team from Vancouver was flown to search area. A Coast Guard PBY evacuated ten personnel. A Navy ground party confirmed taking aboard an injured airman named Vitale Trippodi. ARS arranged to transport a medical team to evacuate Staff Sgt Trippodi suffering from immersion foot.

Op Brix Daily Search Summary, 16 February

At 0816 hours USAF helicopter 2011 departed for Port Hardy. At 0916 Canso 11067 departed Vancouver with 15 Army personnel for ground search party. USN PBY searched Gil Island and Whale Sound. USN PBY and DC-3 searched coastline of Princess Royal Island. A USAF C-82 stood by at Port Hardy with a para-rescue team. McChord Air Force Base despatched Helicopter 6636 to Port Hardy which landed Comox with radio trouble. At 1127 HMCS *Cayuga* reported one injured survivor being brought to shoreline by *Cayuga* rescue team and a shot heard by a third *Cayuga* rescue team. Position report received from *Cayuga*. Injured man found is half mile west of 53N 12910W. At 1622 Helicopter 2011 was over HMCS *Cayuga*. Canso 11067 transported Army search rescue party to HMCS *Cayuga*. Canso 11015 transported Alpine Club team and para-rescue team to HMCS *Cayuga*. Dakota 660 airlifted five barrels of 90 octane gas and dropped them beside HMCS *Cayuga*. Reports received from HMCS *Cayuga* that Lt. C.G. Pooler A02039606 was taken aboard at 1835 suffering from a broken ankle, multiple abrasions and exposure but general condition favourable. In view of anticipated civilian aircraft AFHQ was requested to contact DOT immediately and arrange to have area within 100 miles radius of point 5305N 12910W made prohibited for civilian aircraft until further notice. This was to ensure that civilian aircraft would not interfere with search being carried out in that area. This request was complied with.

Summary of search for 16 Feb. Resue teams from HMCS *Cayuga* landed at first light to search for remainder of missing crew. This included RCAF rescue team, two Army teams and Alpine Club rescue team. It was learned that Lt. C.G. Pooler, USAF, injured with a broken ankle was found at the edge of an uncharted lake by one of the *Cayuga* rescue teams led by Lt. D.E. Rosenroll. Evacuation of Lt. C.G. Pooler to shore by stretcher was so difficult that it took seven hours to travel a mile and three quarters. A *Cayuga* team led by Lt. Morris landed two miles further south and travelled for ten hours

Searchmaster - F/L D.G. Bell-Irving

1   Beginning at 2330 PST 13 Feb ATC informed 12 Group RCC of following received from B-36 aircraft 2083:

    (1) 2330 PST B-36 2075 letting down to lose ice.
    (2) 2335 PST 2075 heading out to sea to lose ice.
    (3) 2340 PST engine on fire - contemplating bailing out.
          Position 5300N 12929W
    (4) 2341 PST lost one more engine. Contact with 2075 was lost
          after these reports.

Flight Plan

2   Aircraft identification 2075. Type of aircraft B-36. Pilot Barry. Point of Departure Eielson Field. Proposed altitude and route 120 R39 B26 A1 Cape Flattery 140 Drct Fort Peck 400 Solonsea Drct Frisco 400 Drct to Destination Fort Worth. Actual time of departure 1627 PST. Estimated time enroute 24 / 00. Hours fuel 28 / 00.

3   There were 17 men aboard. Their names are as follows:

    Survivors:

        Lt.Col. D.V. MacDonald
        Capt. H.L. Barry
        Lt. E.O. Cox
        Lt. R.R. Darrah
        Lt. P.E. Gerhart
        Lt. R.P. Whitfield
        Lt. C.G. Pooler
        T/Sgt M.B. Stephens
        S/Sgt J.R. Ford
        S/Sgt D. Thrasher
        S/Sgt V. Trippodi
        Cpl R.J. Schuler

    Missing:

        Capt. W.M. Phillips
        Capt. T.F. Schreier
        Lt. A. Holie
        S/Sgt E.W. Pollard
        S/Sgt N.A. Straley

Their unit was USAF Base, Carswell Field, Fort Worth, Texas.

Weather

4   The weather in the area during the time of the distress was as follows:

    Port Hardy: Ceiling 2100 ft; sky condition overcast, lower broken;
              visibility 12 miles in light rain; wind ESE 18 mph.

    Cape St.James: Ceiling 500 feet; sky condition overcast;
              visibility 3 miles in light rain; wind SE 52 mph.

Plan of Action

5   A request for all possible air and surface vessel assistance was telephoned to the USAF, USCG and USN. Accordingly four USCG cutters were dispatched to the probability area and full aircraft assistance was provided. (10 USAF long range aircraft, 12 US Navy Neptunes, 6 US Coast Guard aircraft available). A request for a destroyer was telephoned to the RCN. The Cayuga

without finding any traces of the missing men. The third *Cayuga* team led by Cdr. Edwards landed just north of the first team travelled through heavy snow searching the mountainsides to the north and east for 15 hours. No survivors were sighted by this team, but two abandoned parachutes were sighted high in the trees and foot prints were found in the snow. A search team from the Winona landed four miles to the south and covered approximately five miles, while a rescue team from the Cahoone proceeded south. The same distance was made in a northerly direction by a rescue team off the Citrus who landed at the head of Capple Inlet. A nearby mountainside was covered by an RCAF and Alpine Club team. An attempt by a mixed Army and Navy team to reach a parachute reported by an aircraft was unsuccessful because of intervening darkness.

Op Brix Daily Search Summary, 18 February

No results were obtained from ground search parties sent out except for some discarded survival articles and debris found in the middle of a small partially frozen lake near Barnard Harbour. These articles were believed thrown from a plane. Debris was to be investigated the following day.

Op Brix Daily Search Summary, 19 February

The ground search parties all returned with no results except that more equipment was located and brought in. The debris mentioned in 18 Feb summary was a wooden box with radio parts which burst on landing and spread out on a line running north-south 15 feet in length. Interrogation of survivors confirmed that this box had been pushed out of the rear compartment during bail-out. The aircraft heading was thus established.

Op Brix Daily Search Summary, 20 February

The teams from *Cayuga* found a parachute, Mae West and a radar reflector. The reflector was found at the sign of an SOS spelled in the snow. This area had been reported by an aircraft but not previously located from the ground. Fresh snow had obliterated the tracks in the areas.

Op Brix Daily Search Summary, 21 February

Three teams landed from *Cayuga* and searched an area radius 600 yards and centre 5303.75N 12910.2W. One of *Cayuga*'s teams located an unused drinking water kit in the water at the shoreline. More small articles of kit were found in the search area.

Op Brix Daily Search Summary, 5 March

Princess Royal Island north of 5300N was searched using visibility of 3/4 mile 500 feet above ground. Lower scattered cloud prevented complete coverage. Ground search party unable to retrieve parachute today. Search party found radar reflector. Tree will be cut down and parachute retrieved at first opportunity. Search was reduced to following up of possible clues.

Appendix 3: Reports from HMCS *Cayuga*

The command vessel for the sea and ground search and rescue was Esquimalt-based tribal-class destroyer HMCS *Cayuga* (DDE 218), which was commissioned in late 1947 and would go on to serve in the Korean War soon after the Broken Arrow. A month later, the *Cayuga*'s role in the rescue mission was written up in *Crowsnest*, the official monthly magazine of the Royal Canadian Navy, which said, "one of the greatest air-land-sea searches in the history of British Columbia took place in February following the loss of a United States Air Force B-36 over Princess Royal Island." Records from navy Captain M.A. Medland, the *Cayuga*'s commander, reveal the full extent of the mission. His regular report of proceedings of his ship for the period 7–24 February 1950, tell us a great deal about the search for the missing airmen.

"Shortly before 0300 (U) on the 14th, information was [received] by telephone from the Chief of Staff that *Cayuga* would be required to proceed as soon as possible on an Air/Sea rescue mission somewhere in the vicinity of the Queen Charlotte Islands. By 0300 the Duty Watch was preparing for sea and by 0315 steam was being raised in two boilers. At 0730 *Cayuga* reported "Will be ready to proceed at 0815" and in accordance with sailing instructions slipped and proceeded at that time to search for a missing USAF B-36 aircraft No. 2075 ditched in the approximate position 51 degrees 55" North, 128 degrees 20" West."

Cayuga sailed up the west coast of Vancouver Island at high speed and was directed to search the area northwest of Scott Island on the northern tip of Vancouver Island in Queen Charlotte Sound. It arrived just after midnight and took control of the RCAF high-speed launches *Huron* and *Montagnais*.

On 15 February, thirty-six hours after the bailout, *Cayuga* is commanded by radio message at 1345 hours to "proceed to 53 degrees 00' North, 129 degrees 29' West" to pick up survivors who had been rescued by two fishing boats. This was the southern entrance to Squally Channel to the west of Princess Royal Island. *Cayuga* made twenty-five knots and reached the site in two hours and forty-five minutes.

When it arrived, the first thing witnessed by the crew was a PBY amphibious aircraft "taking off with, as understood from the intercepted radio transmission, the first ten survivors." The crew also learned that one injured survivor had been left on the island. Lt. W.M. Kidd, RCN, went to the U.S. Coast Guard vessel *White Holly* to determine the status of the injured survivor and returned to *Cayuga* with enough information to make feasible a last-ditch rescue attempt in the one hour before nightfall.

"At 2100 the rescue team returned to the ship having located and brought out Staff Sergeant V. Trippodi 42271722 USAF. He was suffering from shock and immersion foot but his condition was generally favourable."

The whole operation was done with little coordination and poor communications, so *Cayuga* crew had to make do on their own. By intercepting U.S. transmissions, they learned of the position of the crewmen rescued by the fishing boat and the PBY. They also had Sgt. Trippodi, who provided first-hand details of the bailout. It was Trippodi's information that "set the pattern for the whole subsequent search and though at odds with information received from interrogation of the ten who had been evacuated it was used throughout and was gradually corroborated as the days went by."

It was only on the following day, Thursday the 16th, that *Cayuga* was finally informed that it was directing the land search for crewmen and that the air search was to be coordinated with the land search. This was contradicted by an intercepted message from Seattle, U.S.A., two days earlier that had directed a U.S. commander to take total charge of all operations. As Captain Medland wrote, "During the interval some doubt existed as to how neighbourly this mission was going to be." In the end, the *Cayuga* took command of thirteen aircraft that day and, despite radio difficulties, kept constant control of the direction and pattern of the ongoing search.

Thursday also saw the rescue of the last survivor. "The land search parties covered considerable areas and located and brought out a second survivor Lt. C.G. Pooler A02039606 USAF who had a broken ankle, multiple abrasion and suffering from exposure."

By the 17th, the ship had become a veritable hotel. There were thirty army personnel under the command of Captain Holmes from West Point Barracks, and a combined team of five RCAF para-rescue troops and five members of the Vancouver Alpine Club. A fresh gale was now blowing and Medland said, "The weather was in full control and showed little indication of relaxing its grip." Their other problem was that *Cayuga* was now running low on fuel.

It was only now that search and rescue staff finally determined the true location of the bailout. "The two rescued survivors, the odds and ends of equipment found by search teams and position where the first survivors were picked up indicated that the area to be searched was the three mile deep and five mile long corner of Princess Royal Island adjacent to the anchorage. The first real confirmation of this was received in the late afternoon when a search from [U.S. Coast Guard cutter] *Winona* reported sighting a box of what was thought to be supplies on the ice of a small lake." This was a small area near the western-most coast of Princess Royal Island where Squally Channel opens to Campania Sound. The box was identified as containing "oddments of radio equipment, [and] had been scattered some fifteen feet [5 m] on a line down the middle of the lake." *Cayuga* determined that the aircraft was flying roughly southwest when this box was dropped during bailout.

The weather on Sunday the 19th was poor and worsening. "Lt. Pooler was evacuated by the PBY to McChord Field after what seemed like interminable preparations, concurrences and approval during which time the pilot was obviously unhappy to be on the water with the prospect of having to take off into a slight sea which was on the wake. As if the PBY pilot did not have enough to worry about with the injured man, the deteriorating weather and the commanding officer *Winona* aboard, a strange aircraft arrived and circled in the clouds overhead. At 1540 the PBY aircraft took off to the relief of all concerned." The strange aircraft turned out to be bringing two members of the press.

Fuel for the starving engines on *Cayuga* arrived the next day, and the search was intensified south of the box-on-the-lake location. The RCAF was finally able to supply aerial photographs of the region. The search and rescue specialists on *Cayuga* determined that "the four missing airmen who were known to have jumped first had probably landed in the water between Princess Royal Island and Gil

Island. The fifth missing airman, assuming survival, and that he had jumped later, was thought to have made his way to the south and inland because of the terrain."

Captain Medland and his staff concluded on Tuesday the 21st that "should nil reports be made by the overnight search parties and should still no traces be found after next days thorough search of the northern shore lines, a recommendation would be made to 12th Group RCAF to stand down the ships and personnel of the US Coast Guard, to be followed at a respectable interval by HMCS *Cayuga* whose departure would terminate the active land search."

Medland concluded that "whilst 'Operation Brix' was essentially peace time and passive I have every confidence that in other circumstances one of HMC Destroyers could well act as Headquarters ship for landing parties engaged in a more serious business of finding other people who may in future land on the shore of our West Coast."

At 2100 on Wednesday, 22 February 1950, HMCS *Cayuga* weighed anchor and proceeded for Esquimalt. They fought a gale the entire way home.

Before heading for the beaches, men in charge of search parties were briefed in the "Cayuga's" Operations Room. Lieut.-Cdr. C. R. Parker, executive officer, goes over all aspects of the search, points out areas already covered, assigns new territory to each party and informs them of any new clues that may have turned up overnight. A visual picture of the island is obtained from a number of aerial photos clipped together in sequence. Photos were provided by the RCAF. Left to right are: Petty Officers James Brahan, James Ridout, Jack Strachan and Vincent Mielin. (E-10974)

'Well Done, Cayuga!'

by C.T.

Destroyer Took Prominent Part
In Search for Lost Airmen

One of the greatest air-land-sea searches in the history of British Columbia took place in February following the loss of a United States Air Force B-36 over Princess Royal Island.

The story of the hunt was one of partial success, of failure and of very tough going through the dense bush and over the rugged, snow-covered terrain of the northern B.C. island.

The giant six-engined aircraft first got into difficulties during the early morning darkness of February 14, somewhere over Hecate Straits. With 16 crewmen aboard, the pilot reported he had three engines afire. The plane was icing badly . . . then came the last terse message, "Letting down . . ."

In Vancouver, at 12 Group RCAF Search and Rescue headquarters, the initial moves were quickly made. Flag Officer Pacific Coast was contacted, and by 0815 that morning HMCS "Cayuga," (Capt. M. A. Medland) steamed out of Esquimalt harbor and proceeded "with all dis-

Page four

patch" to search the area of Queen Charlotte Sound and Hecate Straits. Meanwhile, aircraft of the RCAF, the US Air Force and the US Coast Guard roared north to scour the coastline from the air.

The first day of the hunt proved fruitless. Like the search for a C-54 down in the northern Yukon, it appeared that another drawn out and unsuccessful operation was underway.

Then, the next day, came the sudden break. A fishing vessel, the "Cape Perry," sighted smoke on the beach of Princess Royal Island. Closing the island, the skipper saw figures walking on the rocky shoreline. Minutes later came the flash: Survivors from the B-36 had been found.

While the "Cape Perry" was picking up ten of the missing flyers, the "Cayuga" was searching 70 miles to seaward. She was immediately directed to Princess Royal Island.

Also converging on the rescue area were the US Coast Guard Cutters "Winona," "Whiteholly," "Citrus"

and "Cahoone," as well as two RCAF high speed motor launches.

The "Cayuga" arrived off the beach at 1630 that same day and quickly landed a rescue team to bring out an injured survivor reported "hung up" on a mountain side. The position of this man, as reported by the other survivors, was approximate only, and in the failing light the task of this rescue team turned out to be most difficult and hazardous.

Staff Sgt. Vitoli Trippodi, of Brooklyn, had bailed out of the plane, with the rest of the crew, in pitch darkness and over unknown country. He landed in some trees high up on a mountainside. Caught in his 'chute harness, with both legs badly injured, he hung head downwards for ten hours before he was extricated by some of his crewmates who had landed in the vicinity. After cutting Trippodi down from his painful perch, the others were too weak to take him down the mountainside. They had to leave him and make their way to the water.

Lieut. William Kidd, of Vancouver, and CPO E. Wooley, of Langley Prairie B.C., led the "Cayuga's" 16-man rescue squad to Trippoddi's side. Surgeon Lieut.-Cdr. Andrew Weir and Petty Officer Alex Matte, a medical assistant, gave Trippodi a sedative, placed him on a Neil-Robertson stretcher, and made him as

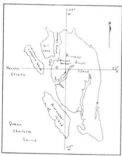

A sketch map of Princess Royal Island, where the rescue operations took place. Spot "X" south of tiny Ashdown Island is where the "Cayuga" and other vessels employed in the search anchored. The circle indicates the general area where Sgt. Trippodi and First Lieut. Charles Pooler were found by "Cayuga" search teams. Search operations were conducted from Surf Inlet to Bernard Harbour and north up Whale Channel, as well as on surrounding islands.

Appendix 4: U.S. Air Force Search and Rescue Report (truncated for clarity)

Commanding Officer, Major Joseph C. Smith

Date 11 APR 1950

Subject

Mission Report (Suspended) (RCS: ARS-CPS-C2A)
Mission Number 4-C-7-13 February 1950.

Nature

At 2345P, 13 February 1950, CAA reported that B-36 AF2075 was in serious trouble. The aircraft was encountering severe ice and engine trouble and was reported letting down over water 53 00'N by 129 49'W. The flight departed 0027Z, 2400 enroute, 2800 fuel, 3-1 pilot, alternate Tinker. There were 17 persons aboard.

Action Taken

13 February 1950. At 2345P, CAA alerted this Flight on B-36 AF2075, reported in serious trouble and letting down over water at 2341P, transmitting on 3105 kcs. Another B-36 AF2083 was in contact with AF2075 and was relaying information thru Vancouver Control ATC. Both aircraft were southbound B-36's. AF2075 estimated over Port Hardy at 028P. At 2347P, operations personnel and the alert crew were notified. At 2355P, CAA reported that the last known position of AF2075 at 2340P, was 53 00N by 129 49'W on a heading of 030 degrees. The aircraft was last in contact with SandSpit Radio.

14 February 1950. At 0008P, CAA advised that AF2083 reported five miles east of Port Hardy at 0001P, 17000' 500 on top and not in contact with AF2075. AF2083 confirmed AF2075's last position. At 0022P, CAA reported that a steady carrier wave was being heard on 3105 kcs by various stations. This indicated that the radio operator on the aircraft may have tied his key down prior to bailing out or ditching. At 0042P, CAA relayed an unconfirmed report from Annette Radio that AF2075 was down on water at 53 00N by 129 02'W. Annette Radio was attempting to determine the source of this information. (At 0105P) Annette Radio advised that they were unable to confirm the source of the message that AF2075 had ditched. The message was believed to be an intercepted transmission between HAM operators discussing the incident, as that had happened in the past. At 0125P, CAA relayed a full report from AF2083 as follows: "Last position I had on AF2075 was at 0730Z as 53 00N by 129 49'W. Pilot said have severe emergency heavy ice, severe turbulence. Am descending down over the sea to underneath and will pick up the coast line and follow coast in by radar. Heading of AF2083 (error which created some confusion as to actual heading of distressed aircraft) at that time was 030 degrees." No one has heard from the aircraft since that time. At 0205P, Flight Service reported that the following had been received from AF2083: "At 2330P AF2075 letting down out to sea to loose ice. Five minutes later lost one engine due to fire. Contemplate bailing out. Ten minutes later lost two more engines due to fire. Lost contact with AF2075 and tried for one hour 40 minutes to establish contact with Port Hardy Radio. Last position 53 00N by 129 49'W." At 0304P, CAA relayed a report that Vancouver Tower was hearing a signal on 4495 kcs. They said that it sounded like an SOS. CAA stated that they had put a good CW man in the Seattle-Tacoma Airport tower. He said the signal was definitely an SOS being transmitted three times and followed by M O, then a figure 52 or 53 which blocked out and the rest of the transmission was unreadable. This was received ICW. At 0325P 12th Group Headquarters, Vancouver, BC informed all agencies that they were assuming operational control of the incident in accordance with ICAO procedures. All agencies were to conduct search as they saw fit but were to keep the RCAF advised. At 0340P, CAA reported that the SOS heard on 4495 kcs is just below the foreign broadcast band, which is heard all the time at night on 4495 kcs. Also at this time,

CAA reported that they had put out a notice to all ships in the vicinity of Queen Charlotte Island and Vancouver Island to be on the look out for the flares, etc as the B-36 aircraft was believed to have ditched in this vicinity. At 0509P, 12th Group Headquarters requested the following: Can you supply a B-36 pilot to 12th Group RCAF as Liaison Officer? At 0538P, Flight Services reported the following information from the 8th Air Force Headquarters concerning the missing B-36: transmitters ART-13 tunable to any high frequency. Frequency used common to coastal route. Receivers BC348, BC453, and ARN-7. No auxiliary power other than normal batteries for communications. Gibson Girl 500 & 8280 kcs. Five and seven man life rafts plus one man life rafts for 16 in crew aboard [This was in error. A check with Eieslon AFB revealed 17 persons]. Rafts carried internally and would be very difficult to remove during ditching. Mae Wests for 16. Pyrotechnics aboard all standard colors. Rations for 2 days for 16 men. Straight and level flight three engines 120–130 miles per hour. All information repeat all information relative to incident will be released through Commanding General 8th Air Force. A weather check at this time indicated low ceilings and rain and snow showers in search area for the next 12 hours. At 0705P, Capt Lawrence Clayton, pilot of a B-36 at McChord at that time, was designated SAC Liaison Officer to the RCAF. At 0742P, Flight Service reported the following information received from Langley Airways: "B-36 May Day water landing between Queen Island sound and Vancouver Island." No frequency was given and Flight Service was requested to attempt to obtain additional information concerning source and frequency. At 0740P, CAA reported that they had contacted several Ham radio operators who stated that Hams all over the country were discussing the B-36 incident. It was believed that the report Langley airways intercepted came from some of them discussing the incident. At 0930P, the RCAF relayed the following ground observers reports from the Queen Charlotte Airlines: A large aircraft was seen near Nimkish Lake near Alert Bay (50 36'N by 129 53'W) at about 2000' headed west at 0012P. A second report was that a large aircraft was seen near Passes Lake also near Alert Bay at about 1000' heading south and apparently in trouble at 0015P. Alert Bay is on the north east corner of Vancouver Island. At 1036P, Lt Richard C. Kirkland departed for Sea Island Airport, Vancouver, BC to act as Liaison Officer to 12th Group and to be in the area in case a helicopter was needed. Lt Kirkland also transported Capt Lawrence Clayton, a B-36 pilot, to Vancouver as requested by the RCAF. At 1446P, Bedford Radio informed this Flight that the RCAF reported a steady carrier wave on 4495 kcs and that they believed it to be a Canadian Radio Telephone Circuit but were unable to take bearings on it as their DF equipment was undergoing an inspection. The Federal Communications Commission was requested to take bearings on this transmission. At 1450P, Brig Gen John B. Montgomery, of SAC Headquarters, arrived at Flight C to observe the mission progress and assist in any way possible. At 1525P, Walla Walla Airways and Seattle Overseas CAA Station reported a constant carrier wave on 8280 kcs with a series of short and long dashes. The Federal Communications Commission was informed and requested to attempt to get bearings. At 1541P, the Federal Communications Commission at Portland, Ore reported that the signal heard near 4495 kcs was calibrated at 4501 kcs and was a Canadian Radio Telephone Circuit using scramble speech. At 1556P, Seattle Overseas Station reported picking up a strong carrier wave again on 8280 kcs. This information was given to the Federal Communications Commission. At 1606P, Lt Kirkland called from 12th Group Headquarters and informed the Mission Commander that the search area for tomorrow was enclosed by the following coordinates: 50 00"N by 127 57'W to 50 00'N by 126 23'W to 48 20'N by 128 02'W to 48 20'N by 123 30'W. This area for search was based on observers reports on Vancouver Island. All stat reported no contact with AF2075 except SandSpit, Anchorage, and Annette radios. Anchorage reported that their last contact with AF2075 was at 0225Z when AF2075 reported leaving Anchorage at 0220Z and estimated Seattle at 0700Z. Annette Radio reported intercepting the following contacts between AF2075 and Sand Spit Radio: At 0604Z position 70 miles SSE Sitka at 0544Z on 4495 kcs. At 0622Z position 20 miles WSW Annette 70 miles NE Sandspit at 0558Z on 4220 kcs. At 0748Z AF2083 reporting for AF2075 reported position 53 00'N by 129 49'W. No further contacts were made. At 1930P, General Montgomery was interrogating the crew of AF2083 in an effort to obtain additional information and clarify some points that were not clear. He also was to call Eielson AFB to check on a report that they heard an SOS on 8280 kcs about the time the B-36 was in distress. At 2130P, the RCAF transmitted a list of ground observers reports, mostly of persons on Vancouver

Island either seeing or hearing a large aircraft "apparently in trouble."

15 February 1950. At 0142P, the Coast Guard informed this Flight that a Mr. Carl Miller reported receiving a series of SOS's on 495 kcs. At 0700P, General Montgomery arrived with complete information as AF2075 as relayed to AF2083. This definitely confirmed the missing aircraft's last position and heading. General Montgomery felt that the crew would bail out rather than attempt a ditching at night. AF2083's track after leaving the area where AF2075 encountered trouble extended over Alert Bay down across Vancouver Island to Tofino and thence to Noah Bay. This may account for the many observers reports in this area. At 0953P, the following was received from the Coast Guard: "Following in reference to SOS's report by Mr. Carl Miller – Several false alerts have been received from this man in the past. He is regarded as very unreliable source and recommend that his reports be disregarded." At 1131P, the following message was sent to 12th Group RCAF: "Following report relayed to you through US Coast Guard 141700P: Eielson AFB reported hearing signals between 0750Z and 1055Z on 6240 kcs. General Montgomery contacted Eielson AFB by phone and correct frequency is 8280 kcs. Radio operators at Eielson believe transmission came from missing B-36 with key screwed down. General Montgomery will explain fully upon arrival." At 1325P, the following message was received from the Coast Guard: "Handle this with care. Just talked with Vancouver RCAF. Two survivors in good condition picked up near Ashdown Island by two fishing boats. That is about all I have no but expect more shortly. Will pass on without interrogation. Again handle this with care. No leaks." At this time Flight Service informed this Flight that General Montgomery's aircraft had landed at Sea Island Airport. It was decided to dispatch the C-82 to Port Hardy to evacuate the survivors that would be flown to the airport by RCAF Canso. F/L Bell-Irving said that the Canso's would fly the survivors to Port Hardy (50 43'N by 127 30'W) where our C-82 would be waiting. At 1348P, CAA informed this Flight that AF1830 had just observed what appeared to be a one man life raft at 48 49'N by 127 13'W. The pilot reported that there was a lot of debris in the area and that he was unable to sight the raft a second time. The debris was not aircraft wreckage.

[Page missing in archival copy]

Due to the confusion created by members of the press and the fact that the survivors were sorely in need of rest, a complete interrogation could not be obtained at this time. At 2310P, the RCAF requested the ARS SA-10 land at daylight alongside the *Cayuga* to evacuate Sgt Trippodi to McChord AFB. At this time 12th Group was advised that SA-10 AF3956 would be over the *Cayuga* at daylight to evacuate Sgt Trippodi. Col Porter, McChord AFB Surgeon, was to attend Sgt Trippodi. Ten survivors were evacuated to McChord AFB and one was aboard the destroyer *Cayuga*.

16 February 1950. At 0015P, the RCAF at Port Hardy relayed the following information they obtained from the ten survivors: "Survivors of the B-36 stated course was being plotted from radar screen steering 303 degrees magnetic as radioed when over Estavan Island 2345P. When in the vicinity of Whale Channel they altered course to 165 degrees magnetic. When three miles inland the order to jump was given and all were out in ten second. The first six out are unaccounted for. The upper winds were from 188 degrees at 47 knots. They jumped at 5000'. Possibility that six missing men are to the north of where survivors landed on Princess Royal Island, Gil Island, or Whale Channel. Careful search by low-flying aircraft suggested." At 0705P, General Montgomery called and requested a thorough interrogation of the survivors as soon as possible. Colonel Reese was contacted and he and Capt Fritz, Flight C Operations Officer, proceeded to the station hospital to interrogate the survivors. By this time (1350P) the destroyer *Cayuga* had reported that one of their rescue parties had located another injured survivor. Cries for help had been heard by a second *Cayuga* party, and shots had been heard by a third group searching the northwest portion of Princess Royal Island. All on the scene search was controlled by the commander of the *Cayuga*. At 1521P, SA-10 AF3956 departed for McChord AFB was Sgt Trippodi. At 1935P, SA-10 AF3956 arrived at McChord AFB was Sgt Trippodi aboard.

17 February 1950. At 0125P, a search summary was received from 12th Group. They reported that Lt Pooler, the 12th survivor to be located, was aboard the *Cayuga* and ground parties from the *Cayuga*

131

and other surface craft on the scene were searching the north west portion of Princess Royal Island assisted by parties from the Canadian Army and the Alpine Club from Vancouver, BC. Aircraft were searching this area, Whale Channel, and the surrounding islands. Cries for help were heard by one party and shots were heard by another.

18 February 1950. At 0615P, an interrogation summary was received from 12th Group. This was obtained from crew members of the ill-fated B-36 as follows: "The heading of the B-36 at the time of bail-out was 165 degrees true. It is probable that the heading during bail-out was constant. The first man jumped at a point 53 12'N by 128 57'W. First twelve from the front section were out in ten second commencing at 0650Z. The five in the rear compartment were out in from five to three seconds. The order of bail-out was as follows: In front Philips (missing), Ascol (missing), Cox (found), Schuler (found), Ford (found), Pooler (found), Whitfield (found), MacDonald (found), Gerhart (found), Trippodi (found), Stephens (found), Darrah (found). The aircraft was navigating by radar at the time of the jump and was obtaining a good clear picture. The wind at the time of the jump was estimated at 190 degrees true at 5000', at 55 knots. It is known that every man left the aircraft. It is believed that every man left the aircraft over land. The pilot was able to see Mount Cardin before abandoning the aircraft. All personnel were dressed identically with mukluks and arctic clothing. No exposure suits were carried. Personnel from the rear compartment carried one man dinghys. No one from the front carried Mae Wests. No E-6 survival kits were carried. The last man out of the rear compartment landed at 53 05'N by 129 07'W. The third man out of the rear compartment landed at 53 04'N by 129 04'W near a frozen lake covered with slush. The first two men out of the front compartment are missing. The third man out of the front compartment landed at 53 04'N by 129 05'W. The last man out of the front compartment landed at 53 03'N or 53 04'N by 129 04'W or 129 05'W. Survivors suggested searching an area around 53 07'N by 129 02'W. They state that they landed in the area with center 53 03'N by 129 02'W and radius six miles."

19 February 1950. At 1655P, the following message was relayed by the Coast Guard from the *Cayuga*: "Lt Pooler evacuated in PBY 254 (Coast Guard) destination McChord AFB."

19 February 1950. Using best information on wind, aircraft track, and height, first man jumping from aircraft could drift to the north at least three miles from position of aircraft at time of jumping. This would indicate high possibility of four missing en landing in Whale Channel. Two of these men were not repeat not wearing Mae Wests or dinghys. There is some doubt of the order on which the fifth missing man left the aircraft.

Joseph C. Smith, Major
USAF Commanding
Flight C
4th Rescue Squadron, ARS-MATS
McChord Air Force Base, Washington
Date 11 APR 1950

FLIGHT C
4TH RESCUE SQUADRON, ARS-MATS
McChord Air Force Base, Washington

MCO   Date 11 APR 1950

File No. _____

SUBJECT: Mission Report (Suspended)
          (RCS: ARS-CPS-C2A)

TO: Commanding Officer
          4th Rescue Squadron, ARS-MATS
          Hamilton Air Force Base
          Hamilton, California

    1. Mission Number 4-C-7-13 February 1950.

    2. Nature.

        a. At 2345P, 13 February 1950, CAA reported that B-36
AF2075 was is serious trouble. This information was being relayed
by AF2083, another B-36 which was in contact with AF2075, and was
transmitted thru Vancouver Control ATC. The aircraft was encountering severe ice and engine trouble and was reported letting down
over water at 53°00'N by 129°49'W. The flight plan was as follows:
AF2075 B-36, pilot Barry, departed Eielson IFR dir Fairbanks 12000
Red 39 Henana Blue 26 Anchorage Amber 1 Cape Flattery 14000 dir Ft
Peck climbing 40000 dir Salton Sea dir San Francisco dir Ft Worth,
landing Ft Worth, true air speed 200K, radio normal VHF, departed
0027Z, 2400 enroute, 2800 fuel, 3-1 pilot, alternate Tinker. There
were 17 persons aboard (see attached loading list).

    3. Action Taken.

        a. Day by day summary of activities.

        13 February 1950. At 2345P, CAA alerted this Flight on
B-36 AF2075, reported in serious trouble and letting down over water
at 2341P, transmitting on 3105 kcs. Another B-36 AF2083 was in contact with AF2075 and was relaying this information thru Vancouver
Control ATC. Both aircraft were southbound B-36's. AF2075 estimated over Port Hardy at 022P. At 2347P, operations personnel and
the alert crew were notified. At 2355P, CAA reported that the last
known position of AF2075 at 2340P, was 53°00'N by 129°49'W on a
heading of 030°. The aircraft was last in contact with Sand Spit
Radio.

        14 February 1950. At 0005P, Personal Equipment personnel

Appendix 5: Other Documents

Joint Committee on Atomic Energy Memorandum on the Incident [truncated for clarity]

SECRET MEMORANDUM FOR MR. BORDEN

March 1, 1950

From: Bill Sheehy

Re: The B-36 Crash

This morning I drafted a letter to General Hall, Office of the Secretary of the Air Force, requesting that we be advised and, if possible, furnished a copy of the report of the Air Force concerning the accident involving a B-36 while on an atomic bomb maneuver. This plane was returning from Eielson Air Force Base in Alaska. I would like at this time to submit this memo as background material for your investigation.

I was making an inspection [14–15 spaces blank] at the time the loading operations were taking place as the initial phase of the Air Force maneuver. Atomic weapons were being loaded into B-50's [46–50 spaces blank] from whence they were ferried to Carswell Air Force Base at Fort Worth, transferred to B-36's, and the actual practice mission or maneuver was planned to fly them from Carswell to Eielson Air Force Base in Alaska and return. I was informed by various people, including the AEC accountability officer, that there would not be a test drop on this maneuver since no items had been requested for expendability. [Deletions in the preceding paragraph likely refer to the AEC storage facilities from which the atomic bombs came before going to Carswell and Alaska.]

Some days later, I received a telephone call from Lieutenant Colonel Wilhoyt, and he advised that they had no official reports from the Air Force but had received verbal reports that the B-36 which went down was carrying an atomic weapon at the time it ran into difficulty. However, the exact details of the disposition of the weapon were not known to him at that moment.

On Friday, February 24, Mr. Heller had a conference with Mr. Shugg, following which he discussed this matter with Captain James Russell, U.S.N., Division of Military Application, AEC. Mr. Heller was advised that the weapon was not detonated in the emergency operations, jettisoning the bomb prior to ditching the airplane.

On Monday, February 27, in accordance with another matter, I conversed with Colonel Skaer, also of the Military Applications Division, U.S. A.E.C., and he advised me that although no formal report had been received from the Air Force, he had been told that the B-36, upon finding itself in trouble, had been instructed to prepare the bomb for a live drop, had gone out to sea, jettisoned the bomb, and then returned over land for the purpose of the crew bailing out and attempting to land safely.

Yesterday afternoon, February 28, I went to the office of Colonel Mills, Air Force atomic energy section, and asked him whether or not we could receive information giving us a "yes" or "no" answer as to whether or not the bomb had exploded, or whether it had been left in the ship to go down with the ship, or just what had happened. General Hall advised that they would like a written request for this information and thought my direct question as to whether or not the bomb had been exploded could be answered before 10:30 this morning in order that the matter might be brought to the attention of the Committee members.

I am not now willing to sit back and wait until the Air Force gets "damn good and ready to tell us what the hell they did with one of our atomic weapons," since this is a matter where we should have some cooperation, and this is a matter of our interest.

WJS (William J. Sheehy)

Addendum:

At 4 p.m. this afternoon General Hall called and stated that he hoped he hadn't caused any inconvenience since the matter had to go personally through the Secretary who is ill, and due to the arrangement for grinding such things out, it had not been possible to call this morning. However, he stated that the information was readily available. I told General Hall that we had briefly stated our interest and advised that further details would be furnished when available. He stated that it was available and that we could get the information. I further told him that the letter which I said would be sent to him was in the mill and should reach him soon.

WJS

SECRET

March 1, 1950

MEMORANDUM FOR MR. BORDEN

From: Bill Sheehy

Re: The B-36 Crash

    This morning I drafted a letter to General Hall, Office of the Secretary of the Air Force, requesting that we be advised and, if possible, furnished a copy of the report of the Air Force concerning the accident involving a B-36 while on an atomic bomb maneuver. This plane was returning from Eielson Air Force Base in Alaska. I would like at this time to submit this memo as background material for your information.

    I was making an inspection_____ at the time the loading operations were taking place as the initial phase of this Air Force maneuver. Atomic weapons were being loaded into B-50's _____ _____ from whence they were ferried to Carswell Air Force Base at Fort Worth, transferred to B-36's, and the actual practice mission or maneuver was planned to fly them from Carswell to Eielson Air Force Base in Alaska and return. I was informed by various people, including the AEC accountability officer, that there would not be a test drop on this maneuver since no items had been requested for expendability.

    Upon my return to Washington, and after reading in the Washington Times Herald the evening of a crash of a B-36 enroute from Eielson Air Force Base to Fort Worth, I became personally as well as officially alarmed. Upon arrival at my home about 7:30 p.m., I made telephonic inquiry to the office of General McCormack, AEC, and was advised by Dr. Paul Fine, who was working in the division at that time, that he knew nothing of the matter and could not give any information.

    The following morning I telephonically contacted Colonel Richard Coiner and asked him if we were interested in the B-36 which had crashed in the Pacific. Colonel Coiner advised that they were not yet certain. It appeared likely and they were going ahead and asking questions of the Air Force in order to get a determination as to whether or not this was one of the planes in which AEC had an interest. Colonel Coiner called me back later in the afternoon and advised me of developments during the day. These developments included the fact that General Wilson had requested individuals stationed at Fort Worth who could do so to give verification as to whether or not the plane which went down was carrying atomic weapons. Colonel Coiner advised that as soon as they heard anything, he would inform me.

    Some days later, I received a telephone call from Lieutenant Colonel Wilhoyt and he advised me that they had no official reports from the Air Force but had received verbal reports that the B-36 which went down was carrying an atomic weapon at the time it ran into difficulty. However, the exact details of the disposition of the weapon were not known to him at that moment. It was following this conference that I first mentioned the matter to you although I had been working on the details of it for more than a week

138

SECRET

CONTAINS DOD CLASS. INFO
COORDINATE DOE, NARA

AUTHORITY: DOE/SA-20
H.R. SCHMIDT, DATE:

AUTHORITY DOE/SA-20
BY H.R. SCHMIDT DATE:

1416

NND 922015-145

SECRET

in an effort to get you an answer which you could present to the Senator, which would cause us no worry or which we might further investigate in order to get the full and complete picture of the situation.

On Friday, February 24, Mr. Heller had a conference with Mr. Shugg, following which he discussed this matter with Captain James Russell, U.S.N., Division of Military Application, AEC. Mr. Heller was advised that the weapon was not detonated in the emergency operations, jettisoning the bomb prior to ditching the airplane.

On Monday, February 27, in connection with another matter, I conversed with Colonel Skaer, also of the Military Application Division, U.S.A.E.C., and he advised me that although no formal report had been received from the Air Force, he had been told that the B-36, upon finding itself in trouble, had been instructed to prepare the bomb for a live drop, had gone out to sea, jettisoned the bomb, and then returned over land for the purpose of the crew bailing out and attempting to land safely.

Yesterday afternoon, February 28, I went to the office of Colonel Mills, Air Force atomic energy section, and asked him whether or not we could receive information giving us a "yes" or "no" answer as to whether or not the bomb had exploded, or whether it had been left in the ship to go down with the ship, or just what had happened. I appreciate Colonel Mills' position and when he took me to General Hall of the Legislative and Liaison Section, Office of the Secretary of the Air Force, I asked him the same questions. General Hall advised that they would like a written request for this information and thought that my direct question as to whether or not the bomb had been exploded could be answered before 10:30 this morning in order that the matter might be brought to the attention of the Committee members.

I have discussed this matter with Mr. Heller on a couple occasions and he feels very strongly that such information, if withheld for any great length of time, might cause some aroused feelings within the members of the Committee if and when presented to them. I agree with this point, but I further feel that the full and complete story must be given at some future date, and apparently the only way we will get it is to ask directly for it.

I feel that the staff of the Committee, at Senator McMahon's direction, and, further, the Chairman himself, leaned over backwards during the investigation of the Jordan case to allow the Air Force all possible cooperation in this matter. I also feel that that was a matter of interest to the Air Force. I am not now willing to sit back and wait until the Air Force gets "damn good and ready to tell us what the hell they did with one of our atomic weapons," since this is a matter where we should have some cooperation, and this is a matter of our interest.

SECRET

NND 922015-146

030040 2

March 1, 1950 memo "Re: The B-36 Crash," page 2 of 3.

SECRET

I therefore respectfully request that you sign the drafted
letter either in your name or that of the Chairman, and put them on notice
at the U. S. Air Force that the McMahon Act specifically states that we shall
make continuing studies of the use, development and control of atomic energy;
further, that we may use the personnel or information of any other Government
agency in carrying out this directive. I think this is a use as well as control
problem and therefore we are vitally concerned and should be fully and currently
informed.

W.J.S.

ADDENDUM:

At 4 p.m. this afternoon General Hall called and stated that he
hoped he hadn't caused any inconvenience since this matter had to go personally
through the Secretary who is ill, and due to the arrangement for grinding such
things out, it had not been possible to call this morning. However, he
stated the information was readily available. I told General Hall that we
had briefly stated our interest and advised that further details would be
furnished when available. He stated that it was available and that we could
get the information. I further told him that the letter which I had said
would be sent to him was in the mill and should reach him soon.

WJS

140

SECRET

NND 922015-147
000050 3

March 1, 1950 memo "Re: The B-36 Crash," page 3 of 3.

Air Force Letter to Joint Committee on Atomic Energy about the status of the bomb:

TOP SECRET

Department of the Air Force
Washington

Office of the Director of Legislation and Liaison
(This document consists of 1 pages. Copy No. 1 of 3 copies)

Mar 17 1950

Chairman,
Joint Committee on Atomic Energy

Attention: Mr. William L. Borden, Executive Director

Dear Mr. Chairman

In accordance with your request of March 9, 1950, the following comments are made with respect to B-36 number 44-92075, which was abandoned by its crew while in flight (3 engines dead and some fire) on February 13, 1950, in the vicinity of Princess Royal Island off the northwest coast of Canada.

Airplane carried an atomic bomb, less nuclear component.

The bomb was jettisoned, presumably over the sea, and it exploded while in the air. Its mechanism was set to detonate the charge at approximately 3800 feet M.S.L.

Since the B-36 story has died out of the Press, and apparently diminished from the public interest, I recommend that no release be made concerning the airplane's bomb load.

We are pleased to be of assistance to you in this matter.

Sincerely,
THOMAS D. WHITE, Major General, USAF
Director, Legislation and Liaison

RESTRICTED DATA
Atomic Energy Act - 1946
Specific Restricted Data Clearance not required
Use Military Classification Safeguards

TOP SECRET
Document No. CXLI

DEPARTMENT OF THE AIR FORCE
WASHINGTON

This document consists of ___1___ pages. Copy No. __1__ of ___3___ Copies

HR-m/96 ......2/19/91

MAR 17 1950

Chairman,
Joint Committee on Atomic Energy

Attention: Mr. William L. Borden
Executive Director

Dear Mr. Chairman:

In accordance with your request of March 9, 1950, the following comments are made with respect to B-36 number 44-92075, which was abandoned by its crew while in flight (3 engines dead and some fire) on February 13, 1950, in the vicinity of Princess Royal Island off the northwest coast of Canada:

The airplane carried an atomic bomb, less nuclear component.

The bomb was jettisoned, presumably over the sea, and it exploded while in the air. Its mechanism was set to detonate the charge at approximately 3800 feet M.S.L.

Since the B-36 story has died out of the Press, and apparently diminished from the public interest, I recommend that no release be made concerning the airplane's bomb load.

[W]e are pleased to be of assistance to you in this matter.

Sincerely,

THOMAS D. WHITE
Major General, USAF
[Direc]tor, Legislation and Liaison

RESTRICTED DATA
ATOMIC ENERGY ACT — 1946
SPECIFIC RESTRICTED DATA CLEARANCE NOT REQUIRED
USE MILITARY CLASSIFICATION SAFEGUARDS

JOINT COMMITTEE ON ATOMIC ENERGY

TOP SECRET

TOP SECRET DOCUMENT NO. CXLI

142

Letter to the Chairman of the Joint Committee on Atomic Energy, from Major General Thomas D. White, 17 March 1950, re: "The airplane carried an atomic bomb, less nuclear componenet. " Top Secret.

Appendix 6: Diary

*Following is an expedition diary by the author covering
27 August–3 September 2003.*

Wednesday, 27 August 2003

South of Meziadin, BC, at the Timber Baron logging camp airstrip.
We arrive at the airstrip at 10:25 am after driving three hours from
Terrace, BC.

The first helicopter load went to the crash site after lifting off at
11:52 a.m. with Mike Jorgensen, James Laird and Mike Carroll for
an expected fifteen-minute flight. Jim will stake out the campsite.
Mike will set up camera shots of the helicopter arrival and departure.

There is no wildlife to be seen other than a mouse or shrew.

All of our cargo went in two sling-loads under the Hughes 500D
egg-shaped helicopters.

It is amazing to think that in a little more than an hour I shall be
at the crash site. This wreckage was once a giant B-36 bomber that
carried a Mk-4 atomic bomb and produced the world's first Broken
Arrow on 13 February 1950.

I have come here as part of a multi-year quest to find out what
happened to that Mk-4 atomic bomb. It was one of the first ever
given to SAC, and they lost it over the Pacific Ocean.

I do not believe that the bomb exists to be found. It was detonated 1 km in altitude over the Pacific to ensure the security of the
design.

What I do not know is what happened to the core? Where is the
6-kg sphere of plutonium and uranium? Since there was a birdcage
(used for the transport and storage of nuclear cores) found in the aircraft crash wreckage, where is the core? The birdcage was presum-

ably empty. The USAF made no attempt to recover the container. Did they recover the core and move it to a new birdcage for shipment?

Since 1954 there have been persistent rumors that a dead body was brought out of the crash site by the USAF in 1954 after they blew-up significant parts of the aircraft. Was it a crewman who stayed with the aircraft? Was it a 1954 USAF soldier who died destroying the aircraft? Who knows?

The helicopter returned at 12:20 p.m. It is a 28-minute round trip over spectacular scenery, about 50 km each way. The helicopter departed with the first sling of cargo at 12:28.

Another great mystery is how did an ailing aircraft with three engines dead and three running, and with ice buildup, and a heavy fuel load, and set to fly SSW, end up in a high mountain area in the exact opposite direction?

Dirk Septer believes that the "fanatical" Ted Schreier stayed on and piloted the bomber to the site. I have trouble with the idea, but cannot discount it as Schreier was never recovered with the other crew. Twelve survived the bailout over Princess Royal Island, and five were lost.

Schreier was said to be the last to jump. Did he or did he not jump? Why would he stay with the aircraft? What would he be doing? Was he protecting something?

I believe that the Mk-4 atomic bomb was detonated over the ocean, and this is a generally accepted version of events.

If the bomb was gone, what would Schreier, the weaponeer, be willing to risk his life in order to save? Was it the core? Was it the Mk-4 bomb? Perhaps the bomb was never jettisoned? Perhaps it was to stay on the aircraft and crash at sea. Maybe Schreier tried to save his bomb. No one would want to be the officer in charge of the first bomb to be declared a Broken Arrow.

We bought $728 of groceries in Terrace. It seems very expensive, but food is dearer in the north. It is also enough for 5–7 days for six men. We will probably be done in three full days of exploration and principal photography.

We are going to have to do lots of airplane archaeology. There are, to my mind now, three basic sections of the bomber to be examined: the bomb bay, the cockpit and the tail. Each will be surveyed and photographed and measured.

We will do a detailed hunt for tools, instruments and bomb-related items.

Also, Dirk wants to hunt for human bone fragments. He believes there is bone evidence of Schreier at the crash site. Maybe. If so, I would be delighted! Such a find would change our view of history, and re-open the question of what happened to the bomb and its components.

Our Prism Helicopter C-GVEB returned to the airstrip at 13:26. A second helicopter arrived at 13:34. I am in now in the cockpit of C-GRYT for the flight to the crash site. The first helicopter is carrying a sling full of cargo. We lift off at 13:41 and leave a minute later. We arrive at the crash site at 14:00, and the cargo arrives two minutes later.

Wow. I can see the wreckage. It is definitely small in appearance. The "USAF" wing marking looks like an upside-down billboard.

The wreckage is strewn all over the ridge. There is very little snow, but some of it must still cover parts of the aircraft. Only three engines can be seen. Nothing is recognizable.

We spend the next hour getting into and out of the helicopter for the film. We swoop and hover and circle. We get in and out. It is all for the film shots of us flying into the site.

We spend two hours setting up camp and tents. Mike & Mike are getting detail shots of the wreckage so that they will not have to stop us while we explore. They arrive back at 17:32.

There is now a discussion of who sleeps in which tent.

I am not convinced this place holds any answers to the mystery. None of the group has been here before.

The peace and tranquility is broken by the generator recharging camera batteries. I look forward to the silence. And to dinner.

What will we accomplish in this desolate place? What will we learn? Will we find anything worth placing in a museum?

19:00, dinner is being made.

20:36, I have crawled up the south scree face to view the camp and the wreckage. Our camp is about 500 m from the main wreckage. My tent is only 10 m from the edge of a snow field. It is so quiet I can hear the snow melting!

Thursday 28 August 2004

08:15, I have gone for a quiet walk NNW of the camp and about 300 m away, and found a remnant of the 1954 [author note: should be 1997/2000] expedition. It is 2.5 m of plastic-coated green cable with intermittent yellow squares in pairs. Two cords are laid out about 10 cm apart, and held down by rocks at 2 m intervals. It is probably detonator cable from the 1954 [should be 1997/2000] expedition to destroy the aircraft. That crash site is perhaps 1 km away. They must have had a very massive amount of cable airdropped.

About 100 m NNW of detonator cord lines I find evidence of the 1997/2000 Canadian Forces expedition. This now makes me think the green cord may be Canadian. I found a wooden box marked "Charges Demolition, UN 0048, 1375 21 845 3271-5603, 40 charges demolition plastic composition C4, 1¼ LB, PCE91H04-07" The NATO number 21 in the sequence means this is Canadian.

10:45, we have walked to the top of the western ridge overlooking the camp and crash site. We three will walk the ridge and peer at mountains and think about the final flight of the aircraft while Mike films us. We finish ridge filming at 12:15.

What is to be learned here? Can we figure out the flight path? Maybe it was not level when it crashed. Maybe it dove into the site. All the snow made it a strange place.

We leave for the crash site at 13:20. From 13:40 until 18:40 we filmed wreckage.

Our first find was a turret with the two guns missing. Nothing was taken for preservation from this already-looted item. The new damage indicated to me that wires had been cut recently and someone had perhaps tried to airlift it out and then dropped it.

Our first significant find was the luggage of an aircrew member. We did not know whom. Many clothes, including dress shirts, toiletries, tooth brush, comb, brush, socks, woolen socks, buttons, and underwear. All was lumped together near the remains of a suitcase.

Only by chance did I discover, in a crack between rocks, the rank insignia. It was the epaulet, and sported a metal leaf. This was a major or Lt. Colonel. The team thinks it was Lt. Col. MacDonald, a survivor of the accident. He was not a regular crew member. The insignia, and its soon-discovered mate, were collected as item #A-2. The toiletries were collected as A-3.

Prior to the luggage, we found the rubber sole of a Bristolite boot. It was collected as A-1.

We moved into the main debris field and found a plethora of objects. This was the rear crew compartment and housed eleven men.

Jim was searching in the receding ice. He found a notebook or diary in the snow. It is wet and could not be opened. It is artifact A-4, and will have to be freeze-dried to reveal the contents.

This part of the aircraft had seats and coffee machines and gun sights and a lot of survival equipment. I saw no fewer than three one-man life rafts, and one immersion suit. Near this was a large white silk parachute in almost perfect condition.

Was this a crew parachute that did not get used? Whose was it? I will probably collect it tomorrow and use it as padding for my cot.

We discover the rear section of the aircraft body is upside down. Why is half of the fuselage upside down?

It is not clear to us which engine is which. The six engines may be scattered randomly, or in an order which should tell of the crash.

The area ahead of the wings, and behind the cockpit, is a total mess. Effects of high explosives and massive fires have reduced vast quantities of the aircraft metal to molten pools on the rocks. Almost nothing is recognizable. There are small globs or balls of aluminium everywhere.

Jim surveyed the nose and cockpit area for radiation. There is lots of residue from the radium-painted instrument dials, which sets off the detector. This was expected and is nothing to worry about.

My most significant find of the day, and a very important nuclear weapons artifact, was the H-frame supporting the bomb shackle and four sway braces, as well as one of the giant bicycle chain hoists used to lift the Mk-4 bomb into the forward bomb bay. It is almost totally intact, but has some melted metal on it, and one hoist is missing. All the sway braces are still in their final loaded position. I would like to recover it.

We finished up at 18:40. For dinner I made chicken tortillas. Everyone had three. Flour tortillas, salsa, onions, green peppers, and spiced chicken. It went over very well. We had Nanaimo Bars for dessert.

Friday 29 August 2003

We are to wear the same clothes so that today's film will be edited in to look like yesterday's film. We will approach the wreckage with the film crew above on the ridge, seeing us arrive at the aircraft.

My plan today is five-fold:
- collect personal and survival items from the rear compartment;
- survey the rear bomb bay which may have contained an extra clip for an atomic bomb;
- recover a conventional bomb clip from bomb bays two or three;
- clear debris away from the H-frame clip behind the cockpit;
- prepare to dig in the snow and ice under bomb bay #1, the home of the lost Mk-4 atomic bomb.

The crew went ahead to film us approaching the wreck. Dirk and I walked in while Jim stayed and fixed camp. He joined us later in the day.

I spent the day collecting and cataloging artifacts from the rear crew compartment and rear bomb bays.

There is a vast amount of personal gear strewn downhill of the bomb bays. There are remains of suitcases, clothes, and a significant amount of survival equipment.

We have found one complete, never used, parachute for a person. Also, several immersion suits still rolled-up, and a couple of one-man life rafts. The remains of at least three survival kits from the rear bomb bay are closely deposited. One is trapped in the rear bay. The rear bomb bays were outfitted for conventional bombing with standard high-explosive ordnance.

The area of the forward bomb bay is completely incinerated. It is a pool of aluminium blobs. No shape remains. The metal melted and formed irregular ingots, globs, blobs, slag, and drips. Nothing of the body or structure in this area can be identified.

Best of all is that somehow the bomb shackle for the Mk-4 atomic bomb survived. It is well ahead of the area where the bomb bay should be. Perhaps it was largely blown clear by the explosions. It still has melted areas, and slag has accumulated.

I managed to remove the very heavy winch from one side, and hope to turn it over tomorrow to view and record the shackle.

This is the best find so far in terms of atomic bomb history. This device held and steadied the bomb in flight.

I accomplished the collection of personal items and survival items from the rear compartments.

I found that the rear bomb bay was equipped with regular bomb racks and survival kits.

I cleared away debris from the atomic bomb H-frame clip.

I dug the bomb bay crew hatch out of the ice near the edge of bomb bay #1. While doing this the funniest incident of the trip happened. Mike was filming me digging in the ice and recovering the crew hatch from the ice. Just as I pulled it out and lifted it up like a trophy, I smelled lemon odour. I said, "I smell lemon. It smells like lemon". Unseen by me, but visible to the sound tech, Igal, was Jim holding up two haves of an orange. Igal was grinning widely, but kept professionally silent while holding back laughter.

Saturday, 30 August 2003
RAIN, rain, rain.

Bad weather. The film crew went for a walk. Dirk and I went to the aircraft. Jim slept.

I gathered and catalogued artifacts such as the bomb bay hatch for the crew; fabric from the control surface of the wings; a navigation compass; electric fuses; a heavy tool; and pressure gauges from the H-frame bomb shackle.

I investigated all the flaps still partially intact, and the screwjacks look to be in a retracted position. The flaps were up, so no one was preparing to land.

The main landing gear crashed retracted, and the nose gear faces towards the nose [the correct retracted position]. The nose gear is upside down.

I may have discovered what they were trying to destroy in the bomb bay area.

Bomb bay #2 contained two shackles used to hold the Grand Slam/Blockbuster massive conventional bomb. Each shackle (x2) had two release clips. All four release shackle points still grasp the lug from a massive object; perhaps a Grand Slam bomb.

Whatever it was, it crashed with the aircraft but did not explode. It is a mystery.

Back at camp I discover in a reference book that bomb bays #2 and #3 carried giant fuel cells to extend the range of the aircraft. These were hung from the major bomb racks, just like the Grand Slam bomb.

Mike C survived a mild bought of hypothermia. Well, maybe not hypothermia, but a very serious chill.

Chicken is roasting for dinner in the camp oven.

We are all very cold and damp. We have been huddling in the main tent.

19:00, all is well. We are all fine and fairly warm.

I think that the aircraft crashed on the top of the ridge and lay in the deep snow. In 1954 the USAF team blew up one engine (#2 ?), and this caused the aircraft to break up and slide down the hillside. Then the team burned/exploded the center section by detonating the fuel tanks in bomb bays 2 & 3. Then lots of burning and small explosions in bomb bay #1 and the forward crew compartment and the cockpit took place.

There is a crater up high where an engine was blown up. I think the giant USAF wing sign is the underside of the port wing. Perhaps when the engine was exploded the wing broke away and flipped over.

The main body slid down the hill and crashed into the engine already blown into that place. The rear (#4) bomb bay survived fairly intact. The rear crew compartment is torn apart and almost totally upside down.

The bomb bay doors are missing, but the opening faces up the side of the hill, mostly upside down. The rear turret area is mostly on its side-to-upside down.

The main instruments seem to be just slightly uphill of the cockpit.

The main area of the burn, to the point of melting all the aluminium and magnesium, is the second and first bomb bays, the forward turret area, and the forward crew area and cockpit.

There is nothing recognizable in bays # 2 & 3; and only the bomb shackles from bays # 1, 2, and 3 survived due to their steel construction.

There are pieces of the bomb bay far up the hill towards the "USAF" wing.

I am spending the evening concentrating on staying warm and dry. Not an easy task. Sun came and went between 19:00 and 20:00.

Not finding the nuclear core Birdcage was a great disappointment. I really hoped (in my active fantasy life) it was still in the wreckage, even though I had credible reports of looting.

The looting is heartbreaking. No one before my team has ever had a license to recover artifacts from this crash site prior to my expedition. Everything prior to this was just theft. Even the Canadian Forces has taken stuff. People from the "Broken Arrow Aircraft Society" in Terrace have looted many many items as proven by the BC Government, which complained about the looting several years ago.

The birdcage is known to be in the United States now.

Sunday, 31 August 2003

SNOW, sleet, rain, cold. The tents blew down

Last night during filming in the main tent, a mighty wind came up and blew down the tent. Mike kept filming while most of us held up the tent. Jim fixed the poles and cables.

By 02:00 my tent had finally collapsed to the point where I was wet. I moved in with Igal, the sound man.

Mike C's tent had blown down the mountainside. The main tent broke its main poles at 04:00

We had intermittent winds from all directions which probably blew 70–90 km/h. Thank goodness we had a wonderful curry-roasted chicken and potato dinner before it all got bad.

Morning was a mix of rain, sleet, snow, with additional wind.

We still have half of the petrol from the generator, and about half a tank of propane for cooking and heating. However, no helicopter will come and get us in this weather. We will have to be patient.

At 14:30 Dirk and I and the film crew went to the suspected site of the 1954 expedition. Far down from the aircraft site, perhaps 1 km, but at least 1.5 km walk, was a site littered with ration cans, bullets, parachute harnesses, and a coffee mug from Heggies in Smithers. This was the 1954 campsite. There was even a glass medicine bottle from a first aid kit.

I collected shards of another Heggies mug, a button, the medicine bottle, a grenade pin, and several bullet shells.

The view from the 1954 campsite is superb. It is one of the most beautiful sights I have ever seen. There is no sound but the waterfalls in the distance. There is no pollution. This is as good as our planet can smell.

17:29, it got more pleasant. There is a light mist, but it is calmer and brighter. Oops, the wind is back.

I would like to photograph the bomb shackle and area once more. I also want to collect some tools from the bomb bay #1 area. Other than these two tasks, I am mostly finished my work here.

Monday, 01 September 2003

Rain, rain, rain, fog, clouds, cold.

It was the worst night so far. All other nights saw fairly good sleeps. Last night I woke up frequently and was cold to the point of shivering. There has been no filming. So far, but we are scheduled to film at 14:00 regardless of the weather. We need to show some of yesterday's artifacts being "found."

Dirk and Jim have gone to the aircraft site. I no longer believe there are significant items to be found at the crash site. All of the tools found so far are common toolbox items.

Imaginations are getting the better of some, and fanciful explanations are offered for unidentified objects.

I have been around these nuclear systems for a long time, and it is my considered opinion that we have found nothing except the atomic bomb H-frame bomb shackle. That I have positively identified.

There is also too much wishful thinking about placement of the aircraft on impact. Dirk has some good ideas, and they are strong because they are simple.

One popular theory is so complex as to be unworkable. It is far too detailed. The grand idea got lost in the details. The attempt to explain everything fails to explain anything.

The bomb is gone. The birdcage was stolen. The "Explosives" detonator suitcase was looted. There is no sign of any atomic bomb tools which can be positively identified.

Only the H-frame survived. And it has NO attachments for

racks or guides for IFI/IFE equipment. This was the earliest and crudest bomb rack available. We learn virtually nothing from the rack other than that it is highly unlikely that the Mk-4 crashed here.

I am not convinced that the direction of flight matters as much as the Broken Arrow event itself. However, it is part of the overall 075 mystery.

Tuesday, 02 September 2003

Today is the fiftieth anniversary of the discovery of the wreckage.

11:21, rain and cloud

Dirk says we are now in "survival mode." There is to be no more filming. Our job now is to stay warm and dry. This would be easy anywhere else in BC. Except for here and Smithers, the rest of BC is clear and 30 degrees. Damn. Of course, it is also burning.

I stayed in my sleeping bag which is quite warm for just over fourteen hours, until I had to pee. Now I will spend some time carding items.

12:35, it is still raining. I have mostly finished carding the artifacts. It has stopped raining for a moment. What a pretty sound. With good fortune we can be airlifted out of here tomorrow.

Wednesday, 03 September 2003

FLY-OUT!! We packed everything, burned some garbage, and awaited the helicopter.

I am finally warm and dry.

Index

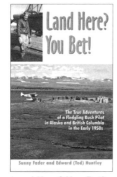
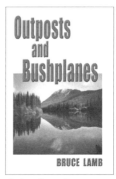

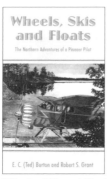
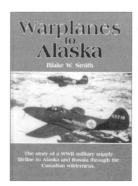
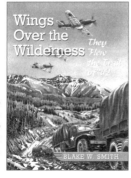